Clifford A. Hauberg

Who's Crazy in this Topsy-Turvy World?

Who's Crazy in This Topsy-Turvy World?

and/or
Liberation Theology versus Christendom

by

Clifford A. Hauberg

VANTAGE PRESS
New York / Washington / Atlanta
Los Angeles / Chicago

Portions of works by Lewis Carroll, courtesy of Crown Publishers

FIRST EDITION

Published by Vantage Press, Inc.
516 West 34th Street, New York, New York 10001

Manufactured in the United States of America
ISBN: 533-04896-6

Library of Congress Catalog Card No.: 80-54108

And as ye would that all men should do unto you, do ye also to them likewise.

—*Luke VI:31*

This book, then, is dedicated to the brotherly spirit of love, mercy and justice that characterized the work of Josephus Daniels relative to the dispute over the oil problem during the presidency of Lázaro Cárdenas

and

The many idealistic students of my St. Olaf classes and especially those who shared the interim trips to Cuernavaca, Mexico, and participated in the elusive search for truth, justice and world peace.

I am a part of all that I have met;
Yet all experience is an arch wherethro'
Gleams the untravell'd world whose margin fades
Forever and forever when I move.
How dull it is to pause, to make an end,
To rust unburnish'd, not to shine in use!

—From "Ulysses," by Alfred, Lord Tennyson

Contents

Foreword, by Frederick J. Bolton xi

Acknowledgments xv

I. The Why and the Wherefore 1

II. Christianity to the Reformation 11

III. Christendom 34

IV. Sanity-Insanity 44

V. Liberation Theology Plus 55

Addendum: Educational Suggestions 78

Notes 83

Bibliography 91

Index 95

Foreword

In this small volume, Cliff Hauberg sketches his reading of European history as it relates to some specific features of the "crazy" present world, especially revealed by Latin American relations. Readers who see that the author wants to stimulate questions and curiosity about the world and how it got this way are "right on the beam." Hauberg is an inveterate question-raiser and stimulator, after years of teaching from secondary school and undergraduate institutions in the United States and elsewhere. His frequent travels abroad, throughout his life, raised questions in his own mind and made him feel stronger through their very presence and power. Questions sensitized him to be a better and more intuitive observer. He wishes the same "disease" to be widespread among a "free people." He distrusts popular certainties and settled powers.

It is not always possible to share Dr. Hauberg's judgments or agree with the particulars of his line of argument. Nevertheless, he does have the wonderful habit of putting his finger on assumptions that need examination or popular wisdoms that presume too much. These are what Hauberg seems to want to bring to light, anyway, and it seems to matter little to him that we do more than let him share his perceptions and insights. He wants others to discover those of his assertions that open the eyes and the mind. Hauberg's wisdom is not always easy, then, but it has arisen as the product of conscientious wrestling with a world he has sought to know on his own terms and not at a distance.

Some readers will notice that, in spite of his iconoclastic tone, he has been deeply influenced by theological discussions of the thirties and forties in the United States, as they gained public expression. Cliff continues to stand by the idea that "The Sermon on the Mount" was a moral discourse and that the heart of the Gospel message was also a moralistic message. Cliff also shares the peculiarly American view that religion and politics can and should be kept apart, though the reader will see places where Hauberg clearly wants to bring them together through a greater common investment in the moral insights planted in "the biography of Jesus."

Some readers will find their eyes boggling as Hauberg claims that the Lutheran Reformers invented the project called "Christendom" and then goes on to call attention to the fact that the Spanish Catholic conquistadores, who knew nothing of the Reformation except as military enemies, brought to Indian America a well-established Spanish ideal of Christendom, which they forced upon the natives. In a longer book, perhaps, such a bold and unusual reading of history might have been filled in for us so that we might investigate it. Hauberg's point, of course, is to agree with Liberation Theologians from Latin America that the Spanish worked a terrible social invasion, which cut the Americans off from their social development. Christendom, as a set of social ideals and structures, was forced upon a venerable society so that it was oppressed rather than finding itself liberated. Hauberg has long perceived injustice and betrayal in any political tactic or strategy that cuts the nerve of indigenous participation in their own affairs. Nonsense is "nonsense" and injustice is "injustice," even when spoken or done in the name of Jesus Christ or His Church. The reader, of course, of whatever creed or persuasion, will find the question rising: "Are *we* also doing that sort of thing?"

With these foreword comments, the reader is invited to "enjoy" in the truest sense of that word. Dig into the assertions and perceptions of Cliff Hauberg for what they may awaken as "points of interest" and "matters for further investigation." Let him stimulate and allow your own increased momentum toward more responsible action. Though the vehicle is a reading of religion and morals, the focus is again in this book on politics and Latin America. Let our ideas behind our political and social relations get some scrutiny. "Wear his shoes and theirs" awhile, and then let your own questions and judgments pour out. Cliff will be pleased.

Frederick J. Bolton, Ph.D.
Associate Professor
Department of Religion
St. Olaf College
Northfield, Minnesota

Acknowledgments

Grateful acknowledgments are made to:

Bramwell House, *Through the Looking Glass* by Lewis Carroll;

Dodge Publishing Co., *The Rubaiyat of Omar Khayyam;*

The Lutheran Standard;

The Minneapolis Star and Tribune;

The New Republic, Inc. © 1980, material reprinted by permission;

The New York Review of Books;

The Saturday Review;

The Washington Spectator.

I

The Why and the Wherefore

According to the almanacs the total population of the world is now approximately four billion. Of that number, one-half live in Asia. In 1975 China had reached a population of almost 850 million with India a close second at roughly 600 million. The Soviet Union with about 260 million, and the United States with 213 million were low by comparison.

In the past, there have been "times that tried men's souls," but as a rule past crises involved possibly only a tribe, a community, state, or the fate of several nations. Since 1945 the situation has been different! In that year, for example, I wrote the lead article for *The Social Studies* as a high school teacher from one of the current hot spots—the Panama Canal Zone.[1] It seemed then that some significant seminal action was imperative by way of world forums or world education to suppress or curb *all* the bias factors which in the past have stimulated the *bête noir* of world understanding—chauvinistic nationalism. Donald M. Nelson had just been sent to China to help in the defeat of Japan with military and technological advice. Then, as now, such help should have been accompanied by efforts to further the enlightened brotherhood of man. Cultural lag in sociology refers to slowness in the rate of development in one aspect of the culture relative to another, as when progress in the nonmaterial fields fails to keep abreast of the technological. Expertise in killing (art of warfare) has so outstripped the concept of world brotherhood (knowledge that should come from home, school, church, and the media) that the present prospects are truly awesome.

Years ago, when teaching at the high school level, I remember seeing a cartoon that appeared on the front page of the popular *American Observer* entitled "Man the Paradox." In the center was sitting a thoughtful person apparently contemplating books dealing with medicine, history, philosophy, agriculture, religion, and so on. Around the circle were props supporting twenty-one-inch cannons ready to destroy the social heritage of the past.

A once popular textbook entitled *The Political and Cultural History of Modern Europe,* Volume II, contains sections entitled "The Promise of the 20th Century," "Enlightened Progress," "Europeanization of the World," "International Cooperation and Peace," and includes, of course, mention of a World Court.[2] According to much civilized thinking, war had been, in the minds of many, relegated to the past or to the benighted areas of the world.

But then came World War I, "the war to end all wars," causing the death of over 10,000,000 soldiers and many civilians in the prime of life. Afterward, the ideals of peace and unity were furthered by the Four Freedoms, the Atlantic Charter, and the League of Nations—the precursor of the United Nations. But we have now passed through World War II—more devastating than World War I—and now the holocaust of World War III looms on the horizon. Why, and For What?

At this point, it might be pertinent to quote the philosophy of the Walrus:

"The time has come," the Walrus said, "to talk of many
things:
Of shoes—and ships—and sealing wax—
Of cabbages—and kings—
And why the sea is boiling hot—
And whether pigs have wings."

Inasmuch as Carroll's poetry has been termed "enlightened nonsense" possibly the above verse provides a proper introduction to the problem of, Why?

Shoes and cabbages may refer to the poverty of the Third

World "have-not" nations. According to Alfred Thayer Mahan, possession of sea power usually meant victory in past wars (ships and sealing wax). Previous to World War II no one envisioned the awful possibilities of nuclear power (the boiling sea and pigs have wings).

At any rate, the world is faced with a problem as ominous as a boiling sea. In 1967 the *Saturday Review of Literature* carried an article "The Nuclear Time Bomb"[3] which pointed out that if the nuclear giants began a bombing confrontation, 75 percent to 95 percent of the civilian population could be destroyed in the countries involved. In this area of man's development there has been "progress." Recent studies substantiate the above prophecy as well as the quote on the cover of the issue referred to:

> If fools and folly rule the world,
> the end of man in our time may
> come as a rude shock, but it
> will no longer come as a—
> complete surprise.[4]

For example, Hans J. Morgenthau in a recent article in the *New Republic* entitled "Fighting the Last War," quotes Albert Einstein thus: "The unleashed power of the atom has changed everything except our way of thinking." In other words, new war weapons are obsolete. As Clausewitz claimed, war was simply "politics by other means."[5] Such is not possible if there is almost total destruction and therefore no victor. Moreover, as long as my enemy has one gun (or missile) that can easily destroy me, why does he need ten or twenty? Presumably the United States has several Poseidon submarine missiles that could wipe out most of the Soviet cities, and undoubtedly the reverse is true. Nuclear power has reduced all-out war *ad absurdum*. World thinking must change. Usually men of all walks of life love the comfortable, the accepted, and have a nostalgia for the "good old days." Originality is often considered instability and we may paraphrase a minor modification of the scriptural parable to read "the bland lead the bland."[6]

Where does the responsibility lie for our obsolescent thinking—home, school, church, or the media? Obviously all must share some part of the blame and a treatment or analysis of the problem, if significant, will of necessity be controversial. Possibly the most difficult factor to treat will be religion. Although the organized church has prided itself on teaching the truth so that people may be free, this has not always been the case. And in a controversy the church has usually had the advantage of speaking *ex cathedra*, i.e., it is wrong to question God or his representatives on Earth as Copernicus and Galileo did.[7]

In the first place, one must doubt and then challenge. Years ago John Ciardi, who then wrote for the *Saturday Review of Literature*, spoke at Saint Olaf College and stressed exactly this point. The purpose of a college course—or a book, for that matter—should not be to provide pat answers to controversial problems, but should arouse serious thinking. This concept of pedagogy probably started with the "Know Thyself" dictum of Socrates but has been emphasized by many profound thinkers throughout the ages. Abelard, for example, in his ethics stressed the importance of doubting and in *Sic et Non* he used 168 chapters to treat dissonant statements from the Scriptures as well as the writing of the church fathers.[8] More recently J. B. Phillips stated in his *Appointment with God*: "It would be dishonest and cowardly to avoid . . . the controversial. A man can only set down what he sincerely believes."[9] Moreover, this treatment will be somewhat similar to Eric Hoffer's *True Believer*. When this book treats such topics as Christianity, Christendom, liberation theology, and especially sanity, it should not be considered an authoritative textbook but rather a book of challenge and thought. Also, it should be remembered that occasionally in the attempt to illustrate a principle or raise new questions it is effective to exaggerate somewhat and sometimes omit a little.

Recently at San Miguel de Allende in Mexico, I heard an excellent talk by Felix Greene on the significance of China. All of his statements were interesting but the one I found most pertinent was the speaker's opinion about the cause for lack of understanding between us of the Western World and the other "worlds." This lack of understanding resulted from the various meanings—or lack of meaning—given such terms as free enterprise, religion, democracy, freedom, liberty, socialism, general welfare, Marxism, etc.[10] A. F. Pollard in his book *The*

Evolution of Parliament introduces a character from Fielding's *Tom Jones* to illustrate the difficulty which may arise because of conflicting ideals in such fields as religion and liberty among people of the same culture. We hear the brash and reverent Mr. Thwackum declaring: "When I say religion I mean the Christian religion and not only the Christian religion but the Protestant religion, and not only the Protestant religion but the Church of England. Orthodoxy is my doxy; heterodoxy is other people's. True liberty is my liberty; other people's is their presumption."[11]

As an instance of emotion-laden or "red-herring" words in all areas of thought the argument between Humpty-Dumpty and Alice over "unbirthdays" and glory is even more striking:

> "But glory doesn't mean argument." [said Alice]
> "When I use a word," Humpty-Dumpty said, "it means just what I choose it to mean—neither more nor less."
> "The question is," said Alice, "whether you can make words mean so many different things."
> "The question is," replied Humpty-Dumpty, "which is master—that is all!"[12]

Along the same lines Henry Steele Commager in his *A Study of History* explains why the subject is often incomplete and confused. Among other factors power distorts. To begin with, at least, the history of the conquistadores was written by the Spaniards, not by the conquered Indians. Justice Holmes is quoted as stating that the "truth" in history is written by the majority vote of the nation strong enough to overpower all others. But, let us pursue further our quest for truth.

Recently, I attended a Methodist church service where the order of worship included the following prayer:

> Eternal God, we confess that we have praised you with our lips but have not glorified you with our lives. Have mercy on us, we pray, for our brief faith that fades under pressure, for our quick enthusiams that just as quickly die, for the hopes we proclaim but do not pursue. Forgive us, Lord God, and give us new trust in your power, that we may live for justice and tell of your loving kindness by

our acts as well as by our words, through Jesus Christ our Lord. Amen.

If such an "evaluation" of school performance were given, parents would demand the resignation of the teachers. Let's "paraphrase" in educational jargon:

The Coach: Look, I've taught you to dribble, block, and the jump shot, but we've lost every game!
The English Teacher: Now we have spent months studying verbs, adjectives, nouns and sentence structure and you still cannot write a paragraph.
The Mathematician: We have studied addition, division, and subtraction, but none of you have the *true* answers.

Homes are in trouble, schools are in trouble, malaise characterizes society in general, and the world faces a holocaust. Something seems to be amiss. If a student leaves high school after four years with the same frame of mind as when he entered, except for a collection of notes and old books, he has escaped education. If a parishioner has attended services for numerous years and is satisfied with the above prayer, he or she also has missed something. To ask the Lord for forgiveness is a spiritual travesty unless it is accompanied by significant action. Forgiveness plays an important role but it should not be used as a cop-out.

Inasmuch as the gap seems to be so wide between achievements that derive from academic and church actions (or *ex cathedra*) more evidence seems necessary to emphasize and clarify the source of the discrepancy. Beginning as far back as the 1940s there have been waves of criticism coming from the populace directed at the public schools. The *New York Times* carried a series of articles followed by Henry F. Pringler's attack in the *Post*, January 20, 1945. The first wave was followed by publications with titles which indicated the wrath of the public: "Quackery in the Public Schools," "Educational Wastelands," and "Why Can't Johnny Read?" More recently some of this criticism has been directed at the higher echelons of learning, especially professors who have been unable to achieve a consensus for reform of our economics and social malaise.

However, if we use historical perspective and glance backward over the last century and a half, we can claim tremendous progress for academia. Once the state of Kansas was considered the northern boundary of the wheat belt. Now wheat is raised as far north as Edmonton, Canada. Furthermore, the yields of all grains has been increased greatly as a result of experimentation in the universities. Norman E. Borlaug, for example, received the Nobel Peace Prize in 1970 for such efforts. Shortly after the turn of the century it was common, especially in the drizzly cold winter months, to see quarantine warning signs of diphtheria or typhoid accompanied by a deathlike skull and crossbones. Today these diseases are almost nonexistent. It even appears that cancer will finally be under control. The achievements in the techniques of construction are truly amazing. Skyscrapers, subways, highways, and space ventures kindle the imagination. These great developments stem from the results of the Industrial Revolution and past scientific progress. But such technological breakthroughs, especially in the area of nuclear energy, must be brought under control. This is primarily a task for the social scientists, but significant moral help from homes, schools, and the churches is imperative. Otherwise, mankind may be approaching the "day of doom" indeed. Social scientists, statesmen, and religious leaders have achieved some progress. *Pacem en Terris, Mater et Magistra,* the Second Vatican Council, as well as the work of the National Council of Churches, are pertinent examples.

Such constructive efforts are often neutralized, however, by evangelistic fundamentalists whose fervent church services and door-to-door preaching are at times contrary to the scriptural Beatitudes—blessed are the peacemakers for they shall inherit the Earth.[13] Change is always controversial and rather than rock the boat it has usually been safer for the preachers, in prayer and sermon, to emphasize that religion is purely an introspective and private matter and not too *significantly* concerned with the current problems of society, national or international. In this respect, it should be noted that the achievements credited to academia are very close "to the least of these" who would like to have more room or say in the world "inn."

Current comment in periodicals seems to substantiate the above point. Under the caption "Silence from the Churches" comes the following quote:

> America's churches are thunderingly silent. I do not suggest that religion should have instant solutions to such problems (world crises, inflation and energy, etc.). Nor is their content so compellingly moral that . . . reticence is a moral sin. But . . . either churches are relevant to society or not; they can't have it both ways.[14]

This point of view is stressed by liberation theology which shall be treated later. Christianity, if it is to be viable today, must live in the frame of current history and not that of the past.

Issues which concern humanity as a whole, such as the fair and just distribution of wealth, energy resources, arms control, and commitment to human rights, to mention a few, should be of paramount concern to those who would shape religious, political and educational activity and thought. Unfortunately, noble ideals and actions have often fallen lamentably short of expectation. Another caption from a syndicated article in the *Minneapolis Tribune* dramatically points to this failure relative to those problems areas of the Middle East and Cuba. The caption reads "Missiles versus Morals: MissilesWin."[15] The churches and other social institutions must concern themselves with the promotion of moral integrity.

The failure to affect the greatest good at any particular time is not an easy problem to solve. We live in a complex age where often the issues are muddled and conflicting. Take, for example, the problem of the equitable distribution of oil. Recently, a very significant issue of the *Washington Spectator* highlighted the tangled interdependency of the oil question. The lead article entitled "A War for the 'Seven Sisters' " reviewed the concepts of a book by Robert Engler, *The Brotherhood of Oil*. After perusing the article one must ponder seriously whether, if a conventional or all-out war starts in the Middle East, it will be due primarily to the holding of American hostages, the Soviet invasion of Afghanistan, the shortages of petroleum, or because the "seven sisters" (Exxon, Texaco, Gulf, Standard of California, Mobil, Royal Dutch Shell, and British Petroleum) wish to regain control of their oil reserves. Until the nationalization moves of the 1970s these giants held at least two-thirds of the world's proven reserves and production of oil, writes Engler. These giants were called "a secret government" by Senator McIntyre and in many ways they dwarfed the military-industrial complex.[16]

It is an axiom of history that those who control and benefit by the status quo usually find red-herring names for those who advocate change needed for the future. Change is inevitable! In this respect, another item from the *Washington Spectator*, "Gleanings from the Congressional Record," is especially significant.

On the floor of Congress representatives stood twenty years ago and finally realized that maybe Cuban dictator Batista wasn't such a great soul after all—but they had never criticized him when he was in power. Contrariwise, these "knowledgeable" men didn't like the way Castro combed his beard. At the outset Castro only wished to enforce the Cuban Constitution of 1940, adopted—but not enforced—when Batista was in power. Nevertheless, this made him a communist threat who had to be isolated.

> He is still in power and most of those who were here and argued that case have long since passed on to the boards of directors of various U.S. firms. Castro is in power today because we isolated him and gave him no choice but to turn to the Soviets.[17]

These gleanings continue to point out that if one wishes to understand Cuba, Nicaragua, the Dominican Republic, Cambodia, Vietnam, and Iran today, it would be necessary to go back and look carefully at Batista, the Somoza family, Trujillo, Lon Nol, Diem, and finally the Shah of Iran.[18]

All that was necessary, in those good old days of the John Foster Dulles tradition, to acquire U.S. assistance, was for a Napoleonic figure to suppress the people and to speak proper Joe McCarthy anticommunist slogans, and aid was forthcoming.

At what point, the gleanings admonish, "does someone, having been hit over the head by a two-by-four, begin to realize that he is making a mistake?" (Senator Paul E. Tsongas, democrat from Massachusetts).[19]

In the 1970s the above comments would surely have justified a critical epithet such as "communist sympathizer" or called forth a Joe McCarthy investigation of the author. But national and world conditions have changed and this warrants characterizing such a person as an enlightened prophet. In this spirit we will treat the topics which follow—Christianity, Christendom, sanity, and liberation theology "plus."

II

Christianity to the Reformation

The Point of View

Writing on this topic reminds one of the story of a group of bankers concerned with the intricacies of the problem of international money. The chairman wished to calm the group by explaining that he had engaged two highly regarded international experts to clarify the problem. But as he pointed out the two experts both disagreed violently. Moreover, what holds for one century doesn't seem to serve properly in the next. In other words, *quod semper quod ubique, quod ab omnibus* or "always, everywhere and by everyone" indicates that the thoughts of the people were the voice of God—*vox populi, vox dei* regarding the concepts of the universe.[1] Ecclesiastically, the Earth at one time was a three-decker affair, flat with heaven above and hell below. Such a cosmology is hardly accepted by enlightened religious groups today. And this illustration applies to many other outmoded beliefs of Christianity.

It has been said that war is too important to be left to the generals and it has already been indicated that the same could be said of education. Change is inevitable in all areas of society and now it appears that the "lay ministry" must become concerned about religion in an enlightened manner. And such interest should not be self-centered or parochial; that is, not just for my pocketbook, my community, state or nation, but for the whole world. About eighteen years ago, John A. T. Robinson fired the imagination of many—layman, ministers and professional theologians—throughout Great Britain and the world by his book entitled *Honest to God*. Naturally a great debate ensued involving all levels of religious thinking. In the sequel which followed, *The Honest to God Debate*, David L. Edwards quotes Paul Tillich to the effect that unity in religion must involve all denominations to a degree greater than many could anticipate. We are reminded that *ecumenical* comes from the Greek *oikoumeme* which means not just "the church" but "the whole inhabited world." Significant action has taken place since, but more serious thinking in this area is long overdue.[2]

The last concept in *Honest to God* is apparently a message from Dietrich Bonhoeffer that "non-religious man" is in bulk a new phenomenon, perhaps not. But what seems to be true, is that many find conventional religion and spirituality completely meaningless, and such individuals will be found among those committed to faith as well as those who are not. We have reached a stage when more significant things are being said openly. According to John A. T. Robinson, such thinking was but a beginning.[3] Grave problems are on the current horizon and time flies. Many letters came to the publisher of *Honest to God*, and many were important and one especially pertinent. Although somewhat critical at the start it points out that the book constituted honest thinking out loud. At the outset Christianity seemed to apply largely to the Mediterranean world, and espoused a rather primitive concept of heaven and hell. A serious crisis has developed because significant developments in such thinking areas as geology (evolution), quantum physics (atomic power), and psychology (witchcraft) have caused "modern man" to reach out for a new pattern of spiritual thinking and awareness.[4]

In preparation for the above comments as well as the remaining chapters, I considered it necessary to refresh myself. First, followed a rereading of much of the Old Testament and essential chapters of the New Testament. Of course, I considered ideas from many of the theologians and philosophers—Karl Barth, Dietrich Bonhoeffer, Reinhold Neibuhr, J.B.Phillips, Paul Tillich, Sören Kierkegaard, Ludwig A. Feuerbach, Bishops James Pike and John A. T. Robinson as well as a bit of Sigmund Freud. My forty-three years of teaching in public and private schools has run the gamut from junior high, high school, junior college, university and finally 25 years at a religiously affiliated liberal arts college. In the latter, of course, I heard and digested, I hope, numerous chapel sermons treating the essence of Christianity.

In my browsing one book seemed to offer great promise in the search for relevant truth, the *Omnipotence of God* by Howard A. Redmond.[5] It included brief summaries of fourteen theologians, eleven philosophers, eleven poets, and sixteen Biblical writers, a thoughtful spectrum from Plato to notable twentieth century thinkers. As far as the relevance of God's power for present day problems, my first reaction was to think of the debates of the scholastic period, twelfth century A.D. The scholastics were apparently belittled for spending too much time on hair-splitting nonessentials; that is—How many angels could stand on the point of a needle? If Lazarus had left a will would it be valid when he was called back from the dead?[6]

Especially disappointing was Redmond's choice of Jonathan Edwards as his number one choice for presenting God in his greatest sense of power and glory. Possibly one had to hear Edward's sermons to appreciate the "great awakening" of the early eighteenth century. Moreover, I can still remember one of my lectures on American history where it was pointed out that to his dying day Edwards was bothered by his inability to absolve the discrepancy between man's freedom of will and predestination. Another puzzling factor that seems to have little to do with omnipotence is that the Calvanistic type of predestination produced in America rugged individualism with a sense of self-responsibility. Such thinking also led to much stress upon education as well as the early establishment of a free press. Whereas in Latin America—with the same God apparently—a sort of predestined fatalism has promoted what one might call individual irresponsibility.[7] This may be noted, for example, in the elite's attitude toward charity and change. The upper class seems to have accepted the idea of giving alms to the poor *por amor de Dios* (for love of God) but seems to have been opposed to doing anything significant about the causes for poverty. This includes also a poor record in the area of education for the *hombre olvidado* (forgotten man). When Mexico, for example, was trying to implement the general welfare constitution of 1917 during the presidency of Plutarco Eliás Calles, this admonition came from the Archbishop of Jalisco:

> What poor are they upon whom God looks with compassion? Certainly not those poor who are discontented with their fate . . . Much less are they the poor who envy the rich only because they are rich and only await the time when they can fling themselves against them with lighted torch or fratricidal dagger . . . with a vehement desire for an unjust distribution of riches. The Savior loves the poor who are resigned and submissive, long-suffering, and patient; who have not put their desires in things of this world, but who try to lay up treasures in heaven.[8]

The above mental maneuvering on the benefits of the omnipotence of God causes one to wonder which of the staves from the Rubaiyat would be the best to follow:

Wast not your Hour, nor in the vain pursuit
Of This and That endeavour and dispute;
Better be jocund with the fruitful Grape
Than sadden after none, or bitter Fruit.

or

A hair perhaps divides the False and True;
Yes; and a single Alif were the clue—
Could you but find it—to the Treasure-house,
And peradventure to the *Master* too—

Probably the best advice here is to follow the first prayer in the frontispiece of *Justice and Mercy* by Reinhold Niebuhr:

> God give us the grace to accept with serenity the things that cannot be changed, courage to change the things that should be changed, and the wisdom to distinguish the one from the other.[9]

Inasmuch as significant changes have and are taking place throughout the world and especially in Latin America we must disagree with the first part of the second prayer: "Nothing that is worthwhile can be achieved in a lifetime. . . ."[10]

In later chapters, especially "Liberation Theology Plus," we shall try to emphasize the importance of current significant developments and agree with the last part of the second prayer that love seems to accomplish much if it precedes dogma, doctrine, or creed. This of course must be true *brotherly* love because during the long period of colonial suffering the church leaders in Latin America—many of whom in the past have thwarted reforms—have naturally professed a "true" faith.

Christology[11]

Now that a point of view has been established for our treatment of Christology we might proceed to a consideration of its origin—the birth of Christ. For the common man it should not be necessary to utilize here the thinking of the great theologians, past and present. Rather, a brief biographical sketch such as what one might find in an ordinary encyclopedia should suffice. When historians require students to memorize such dates as 1066 A.D., 1215 A.D., 1776 A.D., or when the post office stamps a letter directed to any place in the world, the tremendous influence of Jesus Christ is manifest. Undoubtedly Christ has had greater influence on the world than any individual.

Despite his significance for dates, someone apparently made a mistake. He was probably born somewhere between 4 to 6 A.D. The biographies of his life are recorded in Mathew, Mark, Luke, John, and the Acts as well as elsewhere. According to these accounts he was the son of God, sent by the Father, born of the Virgin Mary and Joseph of Nazareth. His coming as a messiah to save mankind was announced by the angel of Gabriel. December 25 is celebrated as the immortal day, but no one is sure of the exact date. His coming was apparently marked by miracles and the angels sang, "On Earth peace, good will toward men. For unto you this day is born a savior who is Christ the Lord." According to Jewish law he was circumcised.

However, it is pertinent to note that peace did not come because his reputation as a savior spread, and the Court of Herod ordered all two years old and under to be killed. Warned of this, the family fled to Egypt for a time. Little is known of the gap between this early period and the later years of his ministry at about the age of thirty.

John the Baptist prepared the way for Jesus by spreading the news of His being a messiah. Apparently Jesus realized He was a great teacher who waxed strong in wisdom and the grace of God. Very early he showed a great love of man and was critical of hypocrisy, driving the merchants and money changers from the temple. He was aided by his first disciples, Peter, Andrew, James and John; later eight more were added.

The second year of Christ's ministry was much like the first although more meaningful in several ways. It is here that we get the Sermon on the Mount with the Beatitudes and the all-important moral principals including the Golden Rule. Moreover, when being questioned by the Pharisees several very significant answers were forthcoming including: "Love the Lord your God with all your heart, soul and mind." This is the first and greatest commandment. The second most important is similar: "Love your neighbor as much as you love yourself." Previously he had said "the God of Abraham, Issac and Jacob is not the God of the dead but the living." Because the faith of some "Christians" is not only bland but sometimes even blind, another quote from Matthew should be included here: "Not everyone that saith unto me Lord, Lord shall enter into the kingdom of heaven; but he that *doeth* the will of my Father who is in heaven." Many also will claim prophesying and great works and I will say unto them: "I never knew you, depart from me, ye that work iniquity."

His last days were characterized by more teaching, significant miracles, and a growing popularity with the common people. His dislike and criticism of the Pharisees in the established church along with its formal ceremony and ritual caused him to be hated by the Jewish church leaders. It was also rumored that he might lead a revolution to establish a Jewish kingdom at Jerusalem. Finally, he was betrayed by one of his disciples, Judas Iscariot, for thirty pieces of silver and arrested. He was tried by a high priest of the Jewish court for claiming to be the son of God. Inasmuch as Palestine was a Roman colony it was necessary for the governor to give the final verdict of guilt. According to some accounts Pontius Pilate was considerate and apparently wished to save Jesus. However, he didn't relish antigonizing the Jewish church leaders so he gave the crowd a choice of freeing one of the two suspects held, Barrabas, a condemned murderer, or Jesus. The crowd which earlier had supported Jesus now in a fickle manner turned against him and picked Barrabas to go free. As a result Christ was nailed to a cross which he was forced to carry to Mount Calvary where he died shortly. Before his death he apparently said to his captors, "Don't you realize that I could ask my Father for thousands of angels to protect me and he would send them instantly? But if I did, how would the Scriptures be fulfilled that described what is happening now?" Inasmuch as Jesus, according to his biographers, knew he was sent by the Father, that he would be betrayed and crucified, the above statement is consistent. But just before his demise he apparently shouted "My God, my God, why have you forsaken me?" After three days in the tomb he rose from the dead and later ascended to heaven.

The last statement of Christ quoted is puzzling indeed. If all was foreordained by God that the Savior came to suffer and die for man and he knew it, why should the term *forsaken* be used. Previously we quoted a passage from Scripture which calls for worship of the Father by not only body and soul but *mind*. If it is not a sin then to have a mind we should consider some of the discrepancies which appear in the New as well as the Old Testament. Futhermore, it is obvious that the material just covered is based on the working of the minds of the biographers and of his writer. Moreover, one wonders—considering the great talent, erudition, and scholarship which characterized the philosophy of the Middle Ages—why it remained for René Descartes in 1641 to produce the concept which might be termed the Magna Carta of modern man, *Cogito ergo sum*, I think therefore I am.[12]

Religion and Dissonant Factors

Religion has been universal. It is doubtful if there has been, in the history of man, even a small tribe that didn't have a form of religion. As a rule a religion has at least three parts or aspects. One is a belief in values incorporated in the minds of the spiritual leaders; namely priests or medicine men. This constitutes a sort of gospel, some collected in a book such as the Bible. Next comes a cult of ceremonies or practices which in Christianity is called the liturgy. Then as tribes or nations become more sophisticated a world view develops which is termed the theology or ecumenism.[13] A dynamic living religion is constantly changing its cult, sense of values, or theology. Only dead religions, such as the mythology of the Greeks and Romans, are static. Therefore, we shall turn from the more positive aspect of this section, Christology, to one which criticizes some material that can be termed useless baggage or myth. For some time now books and articles have appeared treating what some believe should become the dead part of Christianity. This criticism has appeared in such books (already cited) as *Honest to God*, *A Time for Christian Candor*, and *A Gospel Without Myth*.[14] The purpose then is not to destroy but to make a living religion more dynamic and meaningful in the current frame of history, a theme we hope to develop further in later chapters, especially "Liberation Theology Plus." And as Confucius said: "To know what you think is right and not do it is the worst cowardice." We shall therefore treat dissonant statements in both the New (Christology) and the Old Testament. This becomes necessary because Jews have many beliefs basic to Christianity and a person, religiously speaking, cannot be a Christian without being a Jew.[15]

First, a citation from Matthew which reads,

> "For I have come to set a man at variance against his father, and the daughter against her mother, and the daughter-in-law against her mother-in-law. . . . He that loveth father and mother more than me is not worthy of me, and he that loveth son or daughter more than me is not worthy of me . . . And the brother shall deliver up the brother to death and the father the child, and the children shall rise up against their parents. . . ."[16]

It is puzzling indeed that He who is accountable for the Beatitudes, Golden Rule, and the two great commandments should be responsible for such "gospel." Belief of this type could also be responsible for some vicious cults which can hardly be termed Christian. The only sensible explanation is that the biographers were human and subject to error.

Probably the most shocking theologian to appear on the scene in recent years was the late Bishop James Pike, who started out a Catholic, tried being what he called a "humanistic lawyer" and ended up an Episcopal Bishop. In 1966 his picture appeared on *Time* magazine with an article entitled "Heretic or Prophet?" Therein it was pointed out that among other beliefs Pike doubted the truth of original sin, virgin birth, trinity, and the Resurrection. Because Bishop Pike, besides preaching and writing, ran a nationwide TV program his ideas were probably more shocking than others. Additional writers have, however, expressed much the same criticism. David Cairns in *A Gospel Without Myth* and A. T. Robinson's[17] *Honest to God* are written in much the same vein. Moreover, such criticism hasn't brought contempt for the concepts which seem to be essential but now there is more openness. As the article states it has been a long time since the *Trinity* was cocktail-party conversation "but now it is."[18] And after much considering—or reconsidering—most church people have decided that indispensable "myths" are essential for a person's healthy psychic life. However, as Pike and others have stressed there is a need for more *true belief* and less wordmongering and false beliefs. This seems to be true of many concepts in the Old Testament as well as some in the New, otherwise Abelard couldn't have produced a whole volume on such items.[19] Some specific items in the Old Testament can be termed myth and they should be de-emphasized or eliminated because their essential worth is at best dubious. In Genesis (chapters 16 and 17) we have the story of Sarai and Abram and the maid Hagar who became pregnant by Abram at Sarai's suggestion. And the Angel decrees that the bastard son shall be honored. Moreover for these actions Abram and Sarai become Abraham and Sarah at Jehovah's wish. These two are also given a son at 100 and 90 years of age respectively.

In Genesis (chapter number 19) is found the account of Lot and his two daughters who conspired to get their father intoxicated so intercourse would result with them "so our lines will continue." As a result, the two founded two nations, the Moabites and the Ammonites. Exodus 22 is especially concerned with theft, but in chapters 16-19 several types of sexual irregularities are mentioned; for example if "a man seduces a virgin not yet betrothed he shall pay the bride price" and "whosoever has connections with a beast shall be put to death."

One could continue with more of such happenings that involve rape, incest and adultry. Suffice to say that anyone who fails to disapprove of such biblical stories should not criticize Fielding's *Tom Jones*, pornographic shops, or even *Playboy*.

Other concepts are even more open to criticism because they have thwarted or discouraged progress in such areas as astronomy and psychology. In Exodus, for example, we have the statement: "Thou shalt not suffer a witch to live." Apparently both Martin Luther and John Calvin believed in witchcraft and America has suffered the shame of witchcraft with harrassment and death at Salem, Massachusetts, in the 1690s.[20]

In Joshua 10, 12, and 13 statements are made by the "Lord" relating to the sun and the moon that undoubtedly stifled progress in astronomy until the experiments of Copernicus, Brahe, and Kepler led to the discoveries of Galileo.[21]

The story that has had the least appeal because it is so contrary, in application, to what the world needs today as well the essence of the Sermon on the Mount is the account in Genesis 11: 1–9 of the destruction of the Tower of Babel. Here in Babylon, God's people intended to build a large city with a tower reaching to the sky—"a monument to weld them together." This was destroyed because they had begun to exploit their togetherness. And the "Lord" said, "Come let us go down and give them different languages so they won't understand each other's words." This undoubtedly shows ignorance and a jealous nature. Had the writers then possessed today's space-age knowledge they wouldn't have worried about building towers to heaven. Moreover, later in the Gothic period churches were praised because their spires tended to reach heavenward. And more seriously, giving tribes or nations different languages so they would not develop in a friendly manner of brotherly love is quite contrary to the admonition "love thine enemies and love thy neighbor as thyself."

Possibly it would be pertinent to end this section by pointing out that many of those who criticize men like Bishop James Pike and A. T. Robinson agree with them in private but don't like to hear them "burp" in public. Perhaps Jesus himself may see something hypocritical about false teaching: "You try to look like saintly men, but underneath those pious robes of yours are hearts besmirched with every sort of hypocricy and sin" (Matthew 23: 28).

Two quotes from the debate on *Honest to God* point up the problem: "If the whole image we have taught is a myth, it is a myth well worth it, as it has meant decent lives, softened hearts and nations . . . It is like suddenly telling a youngster who believes wholeheartedly in Father Xmas, there isn't a Father Xmas it's your Dad. . . ." Possibly the whole image would collapse. But perhaps this writer never heard of the Thirty Years War, (1618–1648), fought largely over religion and growing nationalism, or the rivalry that preceeded the defeat of the Spanish armada in 1588.

An anonymous reviewer wrote, "Dr. Robinson maintains that the scientific [modern] man can no longer believe the myths and supernatural framework . . . its essentials must be salvaged . . ." but will it be Christianity?[22] The task is apparently one of separating the "kernels from the tares." And it is startling to realize how much unbelief is required to make "belief" possible. And as Eric Hoffer pointed out, at times it seems to be treason or heresy to rely on the senses and reason for evidence of the truth.[23]

Growth of Catholicism

At the outset I pointed out that it would be necessary at times to exaggerate a bit and sometimes omit a little. Such will be true of the story from the death of Christ to the establishment of the powerful Church of Rome.

Considering the long span of history, the teachings of Christ spread rather quickly, all the way from Persia to the Atlantic Ocean. This was most of the world at that time, especially in the history books of the West. Those who did the most to transfer the great teachings of Christ and the power of the church from Jerusalem to Rome were the Apostle Peter and Paul of Tarsus.[24]

Paul was born of a wealthy family and received an education from a great rabbi, Gamaliel. He astonished the Jews by preaching the gospel of Christ in the synagogues. He made three or four missionary trips to the region of Arabia, the Middle East, and Greece, spreading the gospel. Apparently the term "Christian" was first used at Antioch as a result of this missionary work. In later trips along with others Paul travelled to Greece, Cyprus and Asia Minor. On his last trip to Asia Minor he went from Ephesus to Jerusalem and there suffered punishment and a prison term. He demanded a trial as a Roman citizen from Caesar and was sent to Rome. Here he spent some time in prison and during this period of Emperor Nero many Christians were punished. Paul was beheaded about 64 A.D.

Peter was apprently teaching in Rome at the same time and suffered crucifixion as a result, sometime between 64–68 A.D. But Peter's chief significance to the growth and power of the Roman Catholic church is what is known as the Petrine Doctrine.

Peter's given name was Simon, but upon meeting Jesus he was given the name Peter, which means rock. Apparently when Peter affirmed his faith in Jesus as the Son of God Jesus said to Peter:

> Thou are Peter, and on this rock I will build my church and the gates of hell shall not prevail against it. And I will give thee the keys of the kingdom of heaven. And whatsoever thou shalt bind on Earth, it shall be bound in heaven, and whatsoever thou shalt loose on Earth, it shall be loosed also in heaven.

During this period the Roman Empire was beginning to experience many problems and it was therefore a propitious time for the Christian leaders to obtain willing followers. The Church too had its difficulties because the main religious cities, Jerusalem, Ephesus, Alexandria, Constantinople, and so on, vied for leadership. The Arians also caused trouble by claiming that Christ, although divine, was not coequal to God. This was more or less settled at the Council of Nicaea in 325 and finally proclaimed at Constantinople in 381. The heresy was suppressed and the church fathers after this could claim divinity with the Holy Spirit in three "persons" coequal and manifested in one God.[25]

The fall of Rome is usually associated with the "abdication" of the last Roman emperor and the assumption of power by a non-Roman, Odoacer, in 476 A.D. The collapse was more of a "weathering" process. Rome fell but the Romans didn't know it. At any rate the opportunity presented itself for the Roman Catholic church to fill the void left with its own influence and power.

Inasmuch as society during the last years of the great Roman empire seemed to be suffering a sort of social malaise there was an opportunity for the church to grow in spiritual and temporal power, and increase its membership. Because the church had officially been recognized by the Roman government and had vast holdings in a sense, everyone was born willy-nilly into the church during the Middle Ages. Moreover, for a sick society it had much to offer. One book (the Word) defined sin, redemption, and resurrection; that is, immortality given by the one superior son of God in Christ along with the idea of Trinity. In addition, the Ten Commandments, Golden Rule, and Beatitudes offered a code of ethics far superior to any promoted by earlier religions. During the nasty period of the Middle Ages when life was often "brutish and short," the immortality and "storing up of treasures for heaven" must have been appealing indeed. Attractive also was the stress placed upon the role of women in society as well as the concept of the brotherhood of man.

The church seemed to take over the hierarchical type of government from the Roman Empire. At the top the pope, all-powerful, because of the Petrine Doctrine, aided by his underlings in sequence, archbishops, bishops, and priests. Furthermore, because of the sacraments and various doctrinal developments the church really held the power of life and death over everyone from peasant to king or emperor. There were seven sacraments beginning with baptism and ending with extreme unction which dealt with every phase of one's life. Should controversy arise, the leaders of the church could always speak *ex cathedra* (from the chair or authority) and if necessary utilize either excommunication or the interdict. These instruments could be and were used by the pope to refuse or cut off from communion and church membership any person. These could also be used against individuals and nations and during such periods those so punished were often refused the sacraments. The papacy was probably at the height of its power during the reign of Innocent III, 1198–1216, when a dispute with King John of England arose over fiefs and taxes. The pope was able to force the powerful ruler of England to do homage (i.e., become his man) and pay damages to the members of the church.[26] The church, unlike a small kingdom or state at that time, was an undying corporation. It was customary for many individuals to turn over property to Christ's representative before death. Herbert Heaton in his book on the economic history of Europe points out that in many developing states the church owned as much as one-third of the land. After 1000 A.D. it was well on its way to becoming a governor, landed proprietor, tax collector, a material producer and employer of labor on a vast scale, a custodian of morals, a schoolmaster, as well as a compeller of conscience.[27] August C. Krey published an article in the *American Historical Review* entitled "The International State of the Middle Ages; Some Reasons for its Failure."[28] Herein he shows that by the time of Innocent III the church had become an international state, controlling taxation, armies, courts, education, publicity, and diplomacy. From peasant to king it claimed the power of eternal life and death. In summary "Never in history have the moral forces of so vast a society been so thoroughly concentrated and so effective. . . . It is without equal."[29]

Power corrupts and absolute power corrupts even more, especially when too much money is involved. The monasteries did much good work for the church and they usually increased the influence of the pope. The number of such reform movements is significant: the Benedictines in 529 A.D.; the Clunic movement in 910 A.D. and the Cistercians later. The Cluny reform was directed at the abuses of feudalism (especially fighting) but it was also concerned with curbing the aristocratic and affluent living of the upper clergy. For example simony (sale for profit of sacred property) and lay investiture were to be abolished.[30]

There were, of course, other basic reasons for the failure of the all-powerful medieval church, principally, the mismanagement of the crusades (1095–1270s), the rise of the national state, and the tendency of the middle class to begin to support the secular state rather than the Roman church. Inasmuch as society constantly is grasping for universal peace (Holy Alliance, Hague Tribunal, League of Nations, and so on) it is sad indeed that such an experiment in practical idealism had to fail because of greed in the form of personal power and money. The Roman church probably reached the height of its power during the rule of Innocent III, but a century later Boniface VIII the "Vicar of Christ" was unable to enforce his bull *Unam Sanctum* which proclaimed, "We declare, say, and define, that it is wholly necessay for the salvation of every human creature to be subject to the Roman pontiff."[31] Trouble had already arisen between the pope and Edward I of England and Philip IV of France over taxes and power to regulate the national clergy. An indication of the changing times was the calling of the Estates General in France—representing clergy, nobles and the bourgeoisie—to support the king. As a result a backer of Philip IV agreed to go to Italy to capture the Pope and bring him back to be tried and deposed. In this he failed, but with the cooperation of one of the rival "political" leaders, Sciarra Colonna, Guillaume Nogaret was able to break into the Pope's quarters at Anagni. Here the aged pope was humiliated and as a result died shortly afterward in Rome, October 11, 1303. This "Crime of Anagni" marks the beginning of the end of papal control over the secular princes.[32]

Several items must be mentioned before we proceed to the Reformation itself. Furthermore, these amount to basic explanations for the break in the church. Years ago F. S. C. Northrup gave a lecture at my college and he was asked if he believed in a doctrine of absolutes. I have no tape recording of the answer but the reply went something like this: "A doctrine of absolutes without content is not only wrong but sometimes even wicked." Now the Pelagian tendency of good works which the church espoused in the Middle Ages seems to supply what is needed by way of content. So nothing seems to be wrong with the concept of indulgences or good works per se but the *abuses* which were perpetuated are what caused so much criticism. Leo X in March of 1515 announced an extension of an indulgence originally proclaimed by Julius II for the building of St. Peter's Cathedral. Undoubtedly John Tetzel, although he apparently knew the proper church doctrine regarding the merits of Christ, used exaggerated language to cause many of his hearers to give very liberally to the church and for the cathedral. Grants of money for example were declared equivalent to pilgrimages to Rome or Compostella.[33]

Such thinking—or lack of it—seems to come from the church philosophy which existed in the Middle Ages. I have already mentioned the scholastics. Anselm (1033–1109) was their champion who placed faith before knowledge, that is, "Believe and you shall come to know." In other words man's ideas of books, chairs, providence, humanity and so on come from God. To the realists all these were universal ideas guaranteed from above. On the nominalist side, represented by Abelard and Roger Bacon, views could be stated thus: "I know, that I must believe" and "one individual is worth all the universals in the world." Bacon, for example, insisted that in his forty years of listening to the scholastics he had learned nothing. By the same token, one should realize that any doctrine to be significant must acknowledge content. This requires a mind aided by the senses.[34]

The last item before culminating this chapter with the Reformation is the Pazzi plot which involved Pope Sixtus IV and Lorenzo de Medici of Florence and took place in the 1470s. This is touched upon here because it illustrates what was wrong with the church in relation to the changes taking place—that is, the importance of the middle class and the growing nationalism. Sixtus IV was jealous of the growing influence and power of Florence and the Medici family, especially Lorenzo. If Florence should expand it might unite all of Italy and this of course would decrease the secular influence of the church and maybe the Papal States would be taken over. Others who hated the Medici as much or more than the pope conspired with him to eliminate Lorenzo and his brother. Francesco Pazzi, a Florentine banker, Francesco Salviati, an archbishop, and others met with the Vicar of Christ to conspire against the Medici. To the credit of his office the pope insisted there should be an overthrow of the Medici but with no bloodshed. The pope did not insist, however, that no bloodshed meant no plot. A high mass was arranged and at the proper time Giuliano, Lorenzo's brother, was killed with nineteen wounds.[35] Lorenzo, very much an athlete, escaped. A war ensued between the Papal States and Florence for several years.

Both Italy and Germany were united as nation-states much later than the other western states of Europe. This was largely due to the political machinations of the pope with the "Holy" Roman Empire with its seat in Germany and also the Roman pontiff's attempts to thwart the unity of Italy.

Reformation

For the sake of brevity it is necessary again to admit that each of the topics covered warrants at least a volume in treatment. Therefore it is necessary to omit much that is very pertinent and significant.

In the first place it should be pointed out that the Reformation was more of a revolt than a reform. Reform comes later within the Roman Catholic Church itself and in some of the Protestant movements. Hopefully, more reform is to follow. As indicated, the criticism of Martin Luther and others caused many critics to focus on the corrupt practices of the church. Some of which we have already stressed and were of long standing. For example, one may make a list of the items subject to abuse and thus to censure: the power of the pope, wordly living, penance, divine right of princes, faith, and the sacraments. All were criticized by John Wycliffe in much the same manner as Martin Luther—but over 100 years earlier.[36] In the meantime the middle class had grown in numbers and the national state was about to appear in modern form. The spark caused by the ninety-five theses of Martin Luther (1517) split Europe asunder religiously; much of northern Europe was torn from the Roman obedience.

But it would be impossible to understand the so-called Reformation without a few more comments about the Renaissance which preceeded it by several centuries. As indicated, the beginning of Renaissance thinking had shown itself early in England and elsewhere. But with the writings of such men as Dante, Boccaccio, Erasmus, and Petrarch, theological thinking began to change more radically. The rise of the middle class brought a flowering that showed itself in art, literature, architecture, philosophy, and religion. The new man produced did not intend to be bound by the scholastic thought of the Middle

Ages. Even Erasmus—staunch supporter of reform, but only within the framework of the church—ridiculed the scholastic thinking which still lingered. In a letter to his friend Thomas Gray (1499) he satirized, "some pseudo-theologians of our time whose brains are rotten, their language barbarous, their intellects dull. . . . They assert that the mysteries of this science [theology] cannot be comprehended by one who has any commerce at all with the Muses . . . or have drunk of Helicon."[37]

Possible examples of the difference between the old thinking and that of the modern humanistic man would be to compare Saint Bernard and Petrarch.

During the Middle Ages man had lived enveloped in a cowl. Like Saint Bernard [1090–1153] travelling along the waters of Lake Leman [Geneva] and noticing neither the azure of the waters nor the luxuriance of vines nor the radiance of the mountains with their robe of sun and snow, but thought burdened, intent on the terrors of sin, death, and judgments. Beauty was a snare, pleasure a sin, the world a fleeting show. Ignorance is acceptable to God as proof of faith and submission.[38]

But Petrarch, often called the "first modern man," climbed a mountain in southern France for the pure delight of the experience. He loved the flowers, waterfalls, birds and animals, and wrote poems about such things. In other words it might be said that Saint Bernard was typical of the old thinking and loved God in spite of the world; men of the Petrarch type loved God because of this world's offerings. Humanism then was a stage reached where man was not so much concerned with the hereafter with its remote glories but much more with the ever-present *here*, with its pungent life-giving realities. Pico della Mirandola states it very well in his "Oration on Human Dignity": "Other creatures are coericed and limited by divine decree; but man's own decision is the arbiter of his nature."[39] Man was placed in the world so he could better discern what it has to offer. Such a gift of God is man's felicity—let him fly close to God!

Undoubtedly it was time for a significant change as Tennyson has put so well: "The old order changeth, yielding place to new, And God fulfills himself in many ways, Lest one good custom should corrupt the world."

The early humanist had laid the eggs which were hatched by the critics such as Calvin, Zwingli, and Luther. It seems that no historian would disagree with the criticism launched by Luther at the abuses of the indulgences and other examples of pecuniary corruption practiced in the Medieval church. It is unfortunate however that he merely set up one doctrine to replace another, both of which could easily be abused.

Justification of a state of grace achieved by faith alone can be, of course, just as subject to abuse by blind faith as can the improper administration of indulgences and or good works. Moreover, stress on faith only seems to ignore completely the many statements in Christology that call for a worship including *action, being,* and the use of the mind! When Luther claimed the Bible was the sole authority as to God's wishes he was of course denying the validity of the sacraments and the sacredotal system as far as papal power was concerned. Furthermore, when the priesthood of common believer's principle was applied to economic matters in Germany, it lead to the Peasant's Revolt of 1524. Although the demands in the Twelve Articles were rather moderate, such as abolition of serfdom, free hunting and fishing rights, payment in wages for services rendered, and elimination of arbitrary punishment, their rejection caused trouble. As long as the demands were directed at the Catholic lords Luther sympathized; but when the revolt became more violent and threatened the lay lords who were now Lutheran and his supporters he espoused the cause of the princes and begged them to put down the revolt thus: "Whoever can, should smite, strangle, or stab secretly or publickly" these revolting peasants.[40]

The revolt was crushed and later at the Diet of Speyes (1526) and later the principle "cuius regis eius religio" was followed.[41] This has caused several authorities to claim that the major achievement of the Reformation was the achievement of the modern state.[42] What Luther espoused 1517–1530 led directly to what Henry VIII of England did in 1534; that is, he took the place of the pope and the divine right principle was solidified. As far as real reform of the church was concerned, little was done—one doctrine merely replaced another. What had started early with the secular activities of the early Roman Catholic Church had now been brought to a climax. Christendom replaced Christianity and Christology for both Protestant and Catholic nations.

Overall Evaluation of the Reformation

It is a common error to suppose that the Reformation was primarily the work of Zwingli, Calvin, and Luther. Undoubtedly long-standing abuses within the church and humanistic philosophy, as we have already indicated, laid the basis for the break which occurred rapidly after Luther posted his ninety-five theses in 1517. If we read a detailed account of the events which followed it is rather easy to decide that Luther had no idea at the outset of breaking with the Roman church, and Pope Leo X did not expect such action either, as revealed by his comment, "A drunken German wrote these things; but as soon as he is sober he will talk differently."[43] Despite the excitement and commotion caused by Luther's criticism, he did not completely change his mind. In 1518 he again recounted the abuses of which many preachers were guilty but also admitted in the *Resolutions* that they were intended for academic purposes and not to create a new dogma. And although he saw great emnity enflamed against him he would not recant them but did defer to papal wisdom. "I cast myself at the feet of Your Holiness with all that I have and all that I am. Quicken, kill, call, recall, approve, reprove, as you will."[44]

But after Luther's writings were condemned and he was excommunicated naturally the *realpolitick* of the situation changed considerably. Furthermore, when he claimed that salvation came through faith alone and that the Catholic Sacerdotal system was unnecessary, naturally nothing but a rupture could result. Several events made Luther's success almost inevitable: the groundwork of humanistic thinking, the growing nationalism, as already indicated, and the advent of the printing press which could spread the new ideas much faster than before.

In the struggle which ensued in Germany (the Peasant Revolt) it is unfortunate that Luther finally took the side of the princes and thus blessed the concept of divine right of kings. Maybe Luther can be forgiven for this because the previous years had been characterized by feudalistic fighting and he perhaps thought his stand might avoid more bloodshed. Foresight of course indicates that deifying a prince can also lead to abuse. Henry VIII and Louis XIV are rather mild examples, but God-intoxicated "divine-right" rulers can have truely awesome influence—Hilter or Idi Amin for example.

The main Protestant groups at the outset of the Reformation were the Lutherans, Anglicans, and the followers of Calvin. There were more radical movements of a sectarian nature such as the Anabaptists and Mennonites. As a rule these groups wished to discard the old interpretations and doctrines, resulting in more democracy in the church. It seems to me this had an influence of great lasting importance that deserves more emphasis.

After the break with the pope in 1534, the King of England replaced the pope as head of the church, except for the short rule of "Bloody Mary" (1553–58). During Queen Elizabeth's rule (1558–1603), the Catholics were undoubtredly more dangerous than the Protestants to the crown. Many Protestants, however, felt that too much Catholic ritual had survived and wished to purify religious practices—thus the name, Puritans. The Puritans were divided into several groups. Some wished to reform the church from within; others, the Separatists, from without or separately if necessary. One such group, the Brownists, followers of Robert Brown, were the forerunners of the Independents. This group preached that each *congregation* should have the power to settle questions of its own ecclesiastical government, liturgy, and doctrine. This of course amounts to democracy in the church. In principle, this is what Luther's promotion of the principle of the priesthood of the laity did to the Roman church. During the ascendancy of the medieval church, from the fall of Rome in A.D. 476 to the Crime of Anagni in A.D. 1303, the church's power might be characterized as a theocratic dictatorship on a world scale. Those who disagreed with Luther's action probably called his pronouncements religious anarchy which, in a sense, they were. By the same token one who questions the authority of the majesty does the same thing. No institution has been so all pervasive in man's activity as religion and if there was no freedom in church thinking it is hard to see how it could be developed in secular governments.

But let us see just what did happen in England as a result

of the Brownists' activities. Liberal-thinking Independents and Puritans, grouped in parliament, formed the basis for the opposition to the divine right claims of the Stuart rulers from James I to James II (1603–1688).

When James VI came down from Scotland to become James I of England, he was steeped in divine right "wisdom." He was also dubbed the "wisest fool in Christendom." In one of his first encounters with parliament a discussion developed as to some mild reforms in the church. James rebuked the member of parliament for such freedom of speech regarding sacred matters. Immediately he was subject to the Apology of the Commons which pointed out that parliamentary power "capped the 'divinity' that 'doth hedge a king' with a divine quality of the voice that doth issue from the people."[45] The struggle continued throughout the reign of James I, Charles I, Charles II, and James II. In between, of course, the civil wars and the Interregneum took place. During the period of Oliver Cromwell some advance was made in religious freedom.

The Stuart period began with unimpared faith in divine right and the influence of the crown great, especially after the strong Tudors and most particularly Queen Elizabeth. Despite the fact that William and Mary were restored in 1689, the divine right concept died a slow death after these events. In the next century parliamentary government began with Robert Walpole, the first prime minister under the first two Georges. This in turn lead to democracy in Great Britain.

We should have mentioned, of course, that the restoration of the crown (William and Mary) in 1689 was called the "Glorious Revolution" and was accompanied by a bill of rights which included the Toleration Act of 1689. Some historians go so far as to say that the happenings that occurred in England between 1603 and 1689 constitute one of the great revolutions of all times. In a sense, the bill of rights which solidified the changes or gains and was preserved in John Locke's *Essay On Civil Government* served as a sort of palimpsest for what happened in the American colonies from 1776 to 1789. In other words, because Martin Luther promoted the idea of the concept of the priesthood of the laity it was much easier to include in the first amendment to the Constitution of the United States: "Congress shall make no law respecting an establishment of religion, or prohibiting the free use thereof; or abridging the freedom of speech or press; or the right of people to assemble and petition the government for the redress of grievances."

Undoubtedly Luther's proclamations in 1517 were something like the opening of Pandora's box which was supposed to set free innumerable evils, but in some versions of the old myth, the box also contained blessings including hope. Anyone can note the evil associated with blessing the idea of the divine right of secular rulers. Moreover, the Roman church at that time probably considered the other concept—priesthood of the laity—even more pernicious. On the other hand, this concept probably laid the basis for democratic thinking in both church and state and today this development along with love and the brotherhood of man should be the hope of the world.

III

Christendom

Previously we have defined Christology as the theological study of the person, nature and teachings of Christ. Obviously Christianity springs from these factors and is the religion that spread in the region around the Mediterranean Sea, and includes the Catholic, Protestant, and Greek Orthodox faiths, as well as many smaller sects. Christianity also means the state of being a Christian, but what is a Christian? And what then is Christendom? As quoted earlier, Humpty-Dumpty claimed that a word can mean just what a person wants it to mean, no more or less. It all depends on who is master, the person or the word. Therefore let us try to follow the process by which the teachings of the Master became Christianity and then Christendom.

It would appear that as long as the teachings of Christ were largely in accord with the spiritual message of the gospel as recorded by the apostles and others, they were entitled to the term Christianity. But it has been pointed out that those who carried the message were reporters and human personalities; therefore various interpretations, and sometimes disagreements, developed. The Petrine Doctrine is an example of such dissonance. Already we have stressed that religion has been an integral part of all human groups and has permeated all social activity. However, when a large or major part of the Church activity is nonspiritual it is doubtful if the term Christianity is compatible with the message that came from Christ. Previously we have pointed out how very secular were the activities of some of the popes, Innocent III, Sixtus IV, and Leo X for example. We might have started earlier with Pope Gregory VII (1073–1085), whose every move was made with the conviction that he was sovereign in the secular and political realm as well as the spiritual. After the Protestants broke from the Roman Catholic Church, we can see Protestant leaders demonstrating the same concern about political matters. Martin Luther's stand on the Peasants' Revolt is a case in point. The name chosen for this new type of Christianity seems to be Christendom. In order to understand the full thrust of liberation theology, which we shall treat later, it is necessary to delineate more specifically how this development transpired. The term Christendom, religiously speaking, blankets much of the Western World. When the present pope, John Paul II, visited the Western Hemisphere in 1979, the *Saturday Evening Post* carried headlines reading, "A Courageous Pope Speaks Out for Christendom."[1] Inasmuch as non-Christian faith has many moral precepts similar to what is found in Christianity much of what we say about Christendom could apply to non-Christian religions as well. This would be especially true of one part of the Moslem world currently.

It will be our purpose to stress primarily one country (Spain) with occasional reference to others. This is done, first, because Spain, religiously speaking, has been very orthodox and secondly, because it is basic to an understanding of the current liberation theology movement in Latin America and its protagonists. Some of these theological ethicists apparently characterize past and current Christendom as the ideology of the establishment and one feature of cultural imperialism.[2]

People of the United States frequently refer to their country as a unique melting pot. There are very few areas in the world, however, that cannot with justice use the same term. Those that are unable to are the most backward, and Spain has surely not been backward culturally.

Apparently there was a paleolithic invasion of present day Spain about 200,000 B.C. This was followed by a much later influx of a brunette people, the Iberans, about 3,000 B.C. which accounts for the name of the peninsula. From about 1,000 B.C. until Rome destroyed Carthage in 146 B.C., Spain was visited by Phoenicians, Greeks, Cartheginians and Romans. Trade and warfare were the main reasons for these many contacts and, of course, Spain was deeply influenced culturally by them. The Mediterranean Sea had much to do with the early beginning and development of civilization in the West. As a relatively warm body of water, protected on the north by mountains and having connection by means of lake and rivers with surrounding land mass it invited commerce. Three hundred years before Christ the Athenian philosopher Plato said people settled here "like frogs around a swamp." As a result, use of the wheel, horse, and metals (especially iron) became common, along with other cultural practices of course.

After the Punic Wars the Romans dominated Spain more or less until the Moors conquered most of the peninsula in the eighth century. Naturally, the Romans brought their ideas of law, architecture, roads, bridges, language, literature, and finally Christianity. Spain was also subject to barbarian (Vandal, Gothic) invasions from the North during the fifth and sixth centuries. These invading groups absorbed the previous culture so that by the time the Moors came Spain was Christian, at least in name.

In the seventh century, for the first time, Christianity was threatened by a religious rival—Islam, founded by Mohammed. Gradually this religion spread over Arabia and the Middle East, and then over northern Africa. By 710 the followers of Mohammedanism had reached Morocco.[3] Then one of the Visgothic leaders reportedly elicited help—against a rival—from some of the Moors. But he himself was dethroned by his "helpers" and the invasion started, led by the Moorish Chieftan Tarik,[4] who captured Gibraltar in A.D. 711.

There was apparently much confusion and friction in Spain at this time, and by A.D. 718, in only seven years, the Moors had crossed the Pyrenees Mountains. They were able to advance as far as Tours in France where they were defeated by Charles Martel in A.D. 732. Gradually they were driven back across the Pyrenees and this started what is often called the *Reconquista* (reconquest).

Before treating the *Reconquista* in detail it probably should be pointed out that the Moors contributed more to the development of Spain than any of the earlier invading peoples—including even the Romans.

In agriculture the Moors introduced irrigation, fertilization, the science of grafting as well as many new plants including rice, sugar cane, cotton, and mulberry trees (for the silkworm). They were great artisans and Toledo and Cordoba became famous for steel and leather making. Academically they were very creative as they promoted the building of libraries, production of books, universities, and the use of paper. In science also they were far ahead of Europe in their knowledge of chemistry, pharmacy, astronomy, and arithmetic. In religion they were more tolerant than might have been expected as they did not force Islam upon the Christians or the Jews. Wars and commerce may do much to spread civilization. It is probably true to say that the Moorish invasion brought to Spain most or all of the achievements of the Arabs, Syrians, Egyptians, Hebrews, and Greeks. This, added to what the Goths and Romans had already contributed, could have produced a great civilization but then came the *Reconquista*. Before relating those events however we should make a few more comments on the Moslems.

All features of their culture were not superior. The role of women, for example, left much to be desired. Furthermore, it was said that their religion emphasized war and fighting. But maybe this evaluation is a bias of Western nationalism and religion. If, for example, we examine the crusades launched by Pope Urban II at the Council of Clermont (1095) and extending over several centuries, we find ample evidence of Christian warlike attitudes. Moreover, the Third Crusade (1187–1193) reveals the great Arab leader Saladin as the most cultivated and sophisticated character, Moslem or Christian, of the whole crusading period. When Jerusalem finally fell to the Mohammedans there was no pillaging, no slaughter of noncombatants, and Christians were allowed to take with them all their property. Apparently they took full advantage of the privilege and took some property not their own. "Let them alone," said Saladin. "Give them occasion to praise the goodness of our religion." [5] Despite the campaigns of Christian warriors, such as Richard Coeur de Lion of England, Saladin kept the upper hand and even proposed that his brother marry Richard's sister, with Palestine as a betrothal gift! This "modern" proposition was rejected by the Christian leaders. They were lucky to receive a truce that gave them a strip of coastal land and the right of access for pilgrims to shrines in Palestine. Richard the Lion-Hearted now turned homeward (1193) after these slight gains. We cite these events of the Crusade for the reconquest of the Holy Land because they gave us an opportunity to compare them with the *Reconquista* of Spain which runs from the eighth century to 1492, and gives us a chance to evaluate "Christian love" as revealed by the Spaniards.

Reconquista

Although the Moors were easily able to overrun Spain in a short time, they were, as we have indicated, stopped at Tours in 732. With the help of the Franks, led by the great Charlemagne, the invaders were pushed back into Spain as far as the Ebro River by 811.

During this early Moorish invasion period small groups of Christians remained unconquered in northwestern Spain in holdouts in the Pyrenees. In Asturias a lengendary king, Pelayo, appeared and began the drive to push the Moors southward and finally, after Granada fell, into Africa. During this long period of fighting, very interesting developments transpired. At first the struggle was largely a matter of individual leaders, nobles, and clergymen, fighting for more land and it was a rather fitful affair. Then came an event which caused the whole effort to take on the nature of a religious crusade. In the ninth century a bishop claimed to have discovered the tomb of Saint James the Elder—known by the Spaniards as Santiago. Here a church was built and a shrine developed which was visited by thousands of pilgrims. As a result *Santigago y a ellos* (literally, Saint James up and attack them) became the Christian war cry to drive out the hated Moors. Reportedly a bright star came to rest over the tomb in northestern Galicia and the area became known as *compos* (field) *stellae* (star) or in Spanish *Santiago de Compostela*.[6]

During the centuries of the Reconquest there were, however, long periods of toleration on both sides. Mohammedians continued to live in reconquered lands and Christians were unmolested in regions still held by the Moslems. This sort of spirit lasted to the fifteenth century when every Mohammedan became an object of suspicion. This feeling carried over to Jews also because of their close relation with the Moors. During this period, furthermore, the smaller territories developed into larger areas such as Castile and Aragon, and Spain was well on its was to becoming a nation. Symbiosis—to borrow a biological term—developed between church and state. Religion became patriotism of a very orthodox and chauvinistic nature with the chilling war cry *Santiago y a ellos*.

Other developments also occurred which enhanced the power of the growing nation-state. Ferdinand of Aragon and Isabella of Castile, representing two of the largest areas in Spain, were married in 1469. Although keeping their kingdoms theoretically separate, both rulers were very astute and managed to gain control of the military and religious institutions. This was accomplished with the consent of the pope. The rulers also managed to decrease the power of individual cities as represented in the *Cortes* (parliament) and this in turn meant an increase in power for the *Consejo Real* (Royal Council). The Inquisition had also been established in both Aragon and Castile by 1484. In short, by the time *los reyes Catolicos* (the Catholic rulers) launched the last crusade against the Moors who were holding out at Granada it was done in the name of Christianity and the rulers of course, who represented the state. It was a holy war carried out in the spirit of Santiago! Granada finally fell, January 2, 1492, and the pope gave the rulers a silver cross as a result of their victory. Shortly afterward laws were passed which forced Jews and Moors to accept "Christianity" or go into exile. It was a sad event indeed because both Jews and Moors had contributed so much to the culture of Spain in many areas, as we have already indicated. When the grandson of Ferdinand and Isabella Charles I of Spain (better known as Charles V, the Holy Roman Emperor), inherited the throne in 1516, Spain became a truly modern state, ostensibly practicing Christianity.

Inasmuch as liberation theology is much concerned with the system which Spain's old colonialism foisted upon the colonies, it is pertinent to mention how it operated in the New World.[7] Because the early conquerors played such a dominant role in the period immediately after 1492, that stage is often called the "era of the conquistadores." Their escapades and conquests were overall so spectacular, romantic, and remarkable for audacity, endurance, and courage that it is understandable that they are thus remembered. They sought easy wealth for themselves, their king, and their God. Hernán Cortés, who conquered several millions of Indians in Mexico, is possibly the best examplar of the above characterization. Two incidents especially reveal what the *Reconquista* of Spain had done to the thinking of the conquerors and to their culture.

On the way from Vera Cruz to Tenochtitlan (Mexico City) Cortés almost got tricked by the Indians at Cholula. Being very Machiavellian, brave, and also lucky, he was able to turn the tables on the natives. He had acquired an Indian mistress, Doño Marina, who spoke the Aztec language and was able to uncover the plot of the Cholulans. Cortés feigned ignorance of the plot and after the natives were all gathered in the village square about three thousand were massacred to the cry *Santiago y a ellos.* Cortés later captured Tenochtitlan but he had exceeded his authority according to the governor of Cuba who sent Pániflo de Narváez to punish the errant conquistador. This challenge brought out the best in Cortés. Narváez had a force of 800 including 80 horses and 12 guns; Cortés could muster only 250 men, no horses or guns and yet Cortés won! Both being "Christian" warriors they could not use the same war cry. Cortés chose as his symbol the Holy Ghost while Naváez chose Santa Maria. However faith apparently had little to do with victory and the opportunity to exploit the Indians.[8] So much has been written to glorify the exploits of the conquistadores that other aspects of the colonial period are sometimes glossed over or avoided. There were a few brave members of the clergy also. Such a one was Antonio de Montesinos, a member of a Dominican group in Hispanola who used the text "I am a voice crying in the wilderness" and denounced the well-fed congregations for being "in mortal sin . . . for the cruelty and tyranny you use in dealing with these innocent people."[9]

Bartolomé Las Casas was another conquistador, but his start was different. He came early to the New World with his father and acquired a *repartimiento* (a grant of lands stocked with natives to exploit). But he soon realized that the Indians were being abused and was converted, apparently after he heard the preaching of Montesinos whom he later visited. Las Casas was probably the first churchman to be ordained in the New World and dedicated his life after that to working for the good of the Indian. As a result he was called the Universal Protector or "Apostle of the Indians." He finally achieved the promulgation of the New Laws in 1542. These aimed to curb the evils and abuses to which the natives had been subjected. In the regions about the Caribbean he was also active in trying to evangelize the natives by peaceful means instead of by force. He was a forerunner of the liberation theologists because his methods of working with the Indians made a clear distinction between Spanish culture and the true role of Christian missionary activity.[10]

The bishopric of Mexico was established in 1527 and here Juan de Zumárraga also fought for just treatment of the natives. When his secular friends warned him to have less to do with the filthy and poorly clad Indian because he was too old and infirm, his answer was: "You are the ones who give out an evil smell . . . because you seek only frivolities and lead soft lives just as though you were not Christians."[11]

Despite notable preaching and action by some individuals, as well as some orders such as the Jesuits, the New Laws and others were ignored and the Indian exploited. And apparently the natives acquired a rather bad image of church activity in some areas. As Diffie points out the Spaniards were not responsible for the conduct of the Indians prior to 1492. On the other hand, Diffie also claims we can find little evidence that Christianity was effective in raising moral standards.[12] And if we take into account such ethical subjects as lying, cheating, stealing, violence, murder, and other violations of the moral code, the conquerors did not set a good example. In some cases when the natives were told the "Christians" were coming the Indians would fly to the hills with cries of alarm such as "thief, thief" or "the enemy."[13]

Probably no single influence was and is so important in the history of Latin America as religion. It was the all-pervading factor among the Indians before the conquest as it was among the conquerors. But as Dussel points out, Christianity as it came from the "kernels" of Christology should be universal and transcend every culture. A national Christendom seems to subsume elements of Christianity as one element of its culture, and as such seems to have little value for "the least of these." The Jesuits, for example, seemed to have had the proper attitude toward the natives, but they would not take orders from the king. They were expelled from both Brazil and Spanish Latin America by 1767.[14]

To be objective we must point out that such Christendom has not been confined to Spain but more or less characterizes all nation states; a few examples might suffice.

In one of my early years of college teaching a speaker was introduced at convocation time as the foremost authority on Africa. This was long before the emergence of the many new Third World countries of that continent. This lecturer spoke principally about South Africa and the Boers. I do not have a tape recording of the talk but his comments ran something like this: "If you in the United States think your racial situation in the South is bad, it is twenty times worse in South Africa. Moreover, if you think you have religion you should observe the Boers. Many are not satisfied with Sunday Church only but go six or seven times a week. They really have 'faith'—direct connection with the 'Almighty' above. Their culture they consider superior to others and it gives them the right to exploit in a very un-Christian manner humans of other racial types and color."

I have always considered Great Britain one of the most sophisticated and mature nations, culturally speaking. One of the great political and social reforms of all times was the Reform Bill of 1832. G. M. Trevelyan, in his analysis of the opposition to the bill, concludes that the only group that opposed it with any unanimity was not the Tories but the church.[15] This, too, is an example of modern Christendom.

The United States became a world power and an empire as a result of the Spanish-American war (which should be called the Cuban-Spanish-American War). Moreover, the interference in Cuba violated the Monroe Doctrine of 1823, which was once called the cornerstone of American foreign policy. At any rate, because of the trouble in Cuba and the propaganda of United States' media, the American people became "humanitarian." After an overwhelming vote for war by Congress, President McKinley, after much "prayer and hesitation" decided to go along with the voice of the people.[16] War was declared and

Cuba was parted from Spain and "freed." However, the first battle was fought at Manila Bay, as a result the United States acquired the Phillipine Islands for a time. One wonders if orders for this naval action came in answer to McKinley's praying.

Moreover, about a half century later when Third World nations began to emerge as the "have not" areas and the United States began to assume the role of world policeman, this type of foreign policy was often called "piety on the Potomac." Furthermore, religious thinking in the Western World might be characterized by the words puzzlement and malaise.

In *A Time for Christian Candor* Bishop Pike tells of friction arising in a church when a new rector refused to allow a flag procession preceeding the service. Immediately he was criticized by many of the congregation for being unpatriotic and probably a bit communistic. He was told that "the flag has always been used in the service" and "it is done everywhere else."[17] To these church goers such idol worship was an *absolute*. Liberation Theology can—we hope—change this kind of "Christianity."

IV

Sanity–Insanity

When I first contemplated this chapter I planned to entitle it "Insanity." And when one surveys the events which have occurred world wide and nationally, one surely is tempted to use the caption: "Who's Crazy?" Furthermore, psychiatrists analyzing my attempt to very briefly cover this topic relative to religious, ethical, and political thinking surely might question my rationality. Despite the fact that many people are only impressed by thick books and/or fat volumes, I shall attempt to raise doubts and questions in one short chapter.

When a student at a small Lutheran college in my hometown, I had occasion to visit the local asylum for the mentally disturbed. In one section we met an inmate who was sure he was George III of England. When told that this couldn't be true for obvious reasons, he turned and said, "My friend will assure you of the truth, he's Julius Caesar." Later when I attended the University of Minnesota one of the classes I enjoyed the most was psychology. The instructor was excellent and also supplied a stimulating reading program. One small book was entitled *The Psychology of Insanity*. In this book one example of an irrational patient was similar to my previous experience with "George III" and "Julius Caesar." But the book as a whole surprised me because it dealt with daydreams, fantasies, and other commonplace topics. Moreover, the author pointed out that if irrationality was the hallmark of insanity then "It must be confessed that in the present state of knowledge we can offer no completely satisfactory answer to the question."[1] That is, who's sane and who's insane? Hence my ambivalent title to this chapter.

That was many years ago but more recently the same judgement comes from an excellent book, *The Making of a Psychiatrist* by David S. Viscott whose qualifications are very good. Apparently psychiatrists go through a rugged program as resident trainees. On one occasion a goodly number of such trainees were gathered to watch and learn from the "master doctor" as he demonstrated the proper method for questioning a patient. All at once, apparently, the brightest of the group burst out laughing in a hysterical manner. Finally she calmed a bit and stated, "And I thought I'd seen the last of doctors playing childish games when I finished my internship." Everyone seemed to be relieved and the teacher answered, "If you only knew. . . . This is where the real game playing begins." "Yes," answered the trainee, "here you can't tell the doctors from the patients. That's the game, telling them apart."[2]

Doctor Viscott, besides being an expert in his field, also has a keen sense of humor and honesty. In one account he is not above pointing out that the residents in training always sized each other up and worried about who knew the most. They usually acted cool and wanted not to resemble "the idiots they really felt like." Furthermore, Viscott records the conversation and opinion of a regular doctor who stated that he never had experienced a psychiatrist's consultation which was worth a damn. In his opinion it was just a lot of hot air and psychiatry should be taken out of the medical school and classified as archaology or witchcraft.[3] Viscott also contributes the pertinent statement, " 'A pychiatrist knows nothing and does nothing. An internist knows everything and does nothing. A surgeon knows nothing and does everything. And a pathologist knows everything and does everything, but too late.' Look, no one is perfect."[4]

Inasmuch as this quote is found in an excellent book, we should not hesitate to use the kernel of such thinking in an analysis of the problem of world understanding, peace, and religion.

For example, competent scholars in this field usually point out that complexes and rationalizations usually are most evident in spheres of moral conduct which are emotional in nature and of long standing. It is customary to be obedient to traditions acquired from home, class, community, tribe, or nation. If principle and action are not in accord, rationalization ensues and the individual emerges "content." Moreover, this method of dealing with emotional problems is not peculiar to the "insane." Ordinary people often develop "logic-tight compartments" and "dissociation." This makes it possible in all their actions to reveal a sort of Dr. Jekyll–Mr. Hyde personality. It may be possible to prove that such rationalization is untenable, but unless the complex is modified, more rationalization simply takes place. "A man convinced against his will is of the same opinion still." This explains the antithesis between maxim and practice and probably makes it possible to understand a major portion of the human race, sometimes dubbed "conscious hypocrites": "Whose life laughs through and spits at their creed, Who maintain Thee in word, and defy Thee in deed."[5]

If one surveys the world's checkerboard of significant happenings for the last decade or so, one sees much evidence of the above type of thinking and action. Georgie Anne Geyer writes very pertinent articles for the *Los Angeles Times*. One such article was captioned "Contradictory statements make him [the Ayatollah of Iran] unpredictable." She comments on the many statements made by Khomeini to her and other journalists which he later violated or controverted. While an exile in Paris he stressed that the movement to overturn the Shah Mohammad Reza Pahlavi[6] was a religious crusade and no Moslems would be killed. Furthermore, religious leaders should only furnish guidance and not actively participate in secular affairs. In addition, a free press was promised as well as freedom of choice in cultural matters. Since such promises were made, everyone knows the Ayatollah has armed the Moslems, many have been killed; there is no freedom of press or in the area of cultural choice (dress and music for example). Moreover, Khomeini has been the absolute ruler despite his statements that "It [the accusation] hurts me because it is unjust and inhuman to call me a dictator. On the other hand, I couldn't care less, because wickedness is a part of human nature and such wickedness comes from our enemies." When this comment is considered in juxtaposition to the brutal embassy assault and hostage take-over—a violation of international law—one has to see it as an example of one type of mental aberration. In a recent article, an Islamic scholar, Mildred Cantwell Smith, points out that the vehemence and hatred shown by the Moslems must "be understood in terms of a people who have lost their ways, [and] whose heritage has proven unequal to modernity. . . . The Islamic upsurge is a drug not to solve problems but to intoxicate those who can no longer abide the failure to solve them."[7] About the same time President Anwar Sadat of Egypt went so far as to characterize Khomeini's action as that of a lunatic and an insult to humanity and man's honor. Obviously Khomeini's thinking and action is an example of "God intoxication," demonstrating the development of the psychological phenomena mentioned previously as logic-tight compartmentalization or dissociation.

Not only does this characterize the action of some Iranians but apparently the whole Moslem area as revealed by a very recent article entitled "The Myth of Islamic Brotherhood." This religion, like Christianity, emerged from a primitive state of castes, discrimination and abuse of the impoverished. As the Islamic faith developed, its major article of faith was the equality of all men and women before God so that a banker, truck driver, servant, king could all worship side by side. When the author of this article was a little boy, about forty years ago, he was taught in a small village in India that the Moslemic brotherhood of man stretched all the way from the Gibraltar to the Philippines. This was supposed to nuture solidarity and make the people feel stronger and happy. But alas, abuses and friction of class, sect, and nations continued. Today the Islamic world is in turmoil and it is not because of East-West friction or conflicts between industrialized and undeveloped countries. Rather it is antagonisms between the Moslems themselves. For example, because the author of this article's name is Shah and he was born in India, he often was warned by his American friends to wear a button labelled "I am not an Iranian." In his opinion this distinction was quite meaningless when compared to the hostility encountered among any gathering of Moslems. To substantiate this he catalogues the current Islamic friction thus: Algeria and Morocco fighting over oil in the Sahara, conflict between Moslems of Egypt and Libya, clashing between South

Yemen and Yemen proper, which might spread to Saudi Arabia, and hostility between Iraq and Iran and sections farther east of much the same style. An *iman* (priest) characterized the cause for this tragedy in this manner: "Hypocrisy of the so-called Islamic republics that have come into existence today"—from Tunisia to Malaysia. It is not a matter of Jew versus Moslems or the "haves" versus the "have-nots" but "the inability of the Moslems of today to follow the most elementary article of Islamic faith: the brotherhood of man."[8] Is the story of Christendom in the West much the same?

Recently, a local public television station carried a very significant story of the Central Intelligence Agency's actions in Chile and Iran, followed with pictures and documents supporting the contention that we interfered in both countries contrary to international law.

Inasmuch as liberation theology, which is dealt with in the next chapter, claims to have started in Latin America, we shall present the details of the Chilean story more in detail than United States–Iranian relations. Considering the main theme of our book, the story in both countries is much the same except that United States interests have had vast investment of long standing in Chilean copper mines whereas the chief interest in Iran has been petroleum.[8a]

Salvador Allende Gossens was freely elected to the presidency of Chile September 4, 1970, with a plurality of only 36.3 percent largely coming from a coalition vote of the socialist and communist parties of Chile. Shortly after election, Allende renewed diplomatic relations with Cuba and erected a statue honoring Ernesto (Ché) Guevara, who had aided Cuba's Castro and was later killed fighting for reforms for the lower classes in Bolivia. The United States' Central Intelligence Agency aid was directly responsible for elimination of Guevara in Bolivia.[9]

Three years later a military coup overthrew Allende and he was succeeded by a military junta headed by General Augusto Pinochet. The reason given for the overthrow by the rightest element was that Allende's nationalizations were unconstitutional because Allende did not have a mandate from the people—only a 36.6 percent plurality.

There was probably not too much opposition to Allende's first moves to nationalize copper, petroleum, iron, and nitrates because they were largely foreign owned. The early years of the administration were marked by high inflation and a general economic and social crisis. When further nationalization was threatened including farm and factory property, some at least owned by Chileans, the middle class supposedly joined the movement to depose Allende. Such is the account found in encyclopedias. No mention is made in such publications of CIA interference from the late sixties to the final overthrow. According to the public broadcasting channel mentioned above, as well as other reports, the CIA was actively in Chile before the election of 1970, trying to prevent Allende's election. Possibly over ten million dollars was spent on such action and fomenting social and economic discontent. Allende, then, was overthrown not so much because of his ineptness at government but because of CIA interference which was contrary to precepts of the Organization of American States and the United Nations. Some even feel that the death of Allende was not a suicide but should be laid at the door of the United States. It should be remembered that he was trying to promote the welfare of the "least of these" and not the "money changers."

The public broadcasting program mentioned above dealt not only with Chile but also the Central Intelligence Agency's actions in Iran in support of the Shah, who was overthrown by Khomeini. Earlier in the year (1980) *60 Minutes* on CBS catalogued the cruel and repressive nature of the Shah's attempts to reform Iran, and the Cental Intelligence Agency's involvement. This is substantiated by an article in the *Minneapolis Star* based on observations by Donald Fraser—then Mayor-elect of Minneapolis—who is considered an expert on Iran because of his long service on the United States House of Representatives Foreign Affairs Committee. Anti-Shah sources estimate that the number killed during his reign is somewhere between 25,000 and 100,000. Naturally our state department figures are much lower—2,800 to 3,500. Judging by the size of SAVAK (the 50,000-member secret police force of the Shah) the number killed during this period must have been very large, and the torture cruel. Many were subject to not only beatings and electric shock but "also insertion of a bottle in the rectum, hanging weights from testicles, ropes, and such apparatus as a helmet that worn over the head of a victim, magnifies his own screams." The Shah in his attempt to modernize Iran did not spare either Khomeini's Moslem supporters or the Marxist dissidents. Fraser as chairman of the House Subcommittee on International Relations termed the evidence against SAVAK and the Shah as "very serious." He added in the interview that the Shah was not in the same league with Hitler or Idi Amin of Uganda.[10] Should this characterization be any consolation for the Shah or those who aided the Shah? Possibly Ramsey Clark (former United States' Attorney General) is a voice "crying in the wilderness" and possibly right in making his claim, after his recent visit to Iran (May–June 1980), that the United States was wrong in aiding the Shah and should apologize. Also Moslems and Christians alike might sincerely ask themselves: Who's Christians in a truly Christological sense, inasmuch as Moslems acknowledge Christ as a prophet.

Other happenings of the last decade or so seem to cry out for something better than what present day Christendom, Mohammedanism or other religions seem to offer.

Probably the worst of these is the nightmare in Jonestown (Guyana) where Congressman Leo Ryan, three newsmen, and 900 followers of Jim Jones died in the name of religion in the fall of 1978. According to an article in *Time,* Jones was born an Indiana humanitarian but degenerated into an egomaniac. Psychologists must ponder the explanation for what turned "an idyllic haven from modern society into a hellish colony of death." Probably the answer can be found in the comments of Dostoyevsky (quoted) as well as psychologists in an article in *Time* entitled the "Cult of Death." Herein it is pointed out that many people have a pressing need to find somebody to whom they can surrender and apparently Jim Jones took the place of God. This means the individual relinquishes the God given freedom to make his own choices and face realities. Many, therefore, chose death because it had already been proclaimed as a sort of rebirth.[11]

Another event which points up the same weakness in society is Scientology. On April 13, 1980, *60 Minutes* exposed the characteristics of such a group operating in a Florida town. As portrayed, the leaders admitted to serious violations of the Ten Commandments in attempts to destroy those who wished to investigate them for possible fraud—all done in the name of religion.

Possibly just as pertinent or even more serious are the "pop" style crusades for Christ because they touch more people. Before I "witnessed" the last one, I read an article entitled "The Conversion of Billy Graham." It was pointed out that Graham was the father confessor of Lyndon Johnson and court chaplain to Richard Nixon. And it should be stressed that this was true of the years that accounted for Vietnam War, Watergate, and the machinations in Chile and Iran. According to the article the tone of the convert maker is now different. He is for peace, disarmament, and criticized President Truman for dropping the first atomic bomb. Furthermore, the coexistence of church and state had supposedly opened Graham's eyes to the dangers of a nuclear East-West holocaust. However, what I saw on one recent program (June 1980) was very much a "Hollywood" affair of pretty girls singing religious songs and many snaps of be-medalled generals, apparently captivated by the patriotic church-state aspect of the program and the promise of "treasures in heaven." So probably the newspaper article is right in being a bit skeptical of the naive "Bible-thumper," because Graham's flock does not seem to have too much passion for what makes for world understanding and consequently the possibility of peace. Does he dare to offend them?[12]

Inasmuch as some people might take umbrage at criticism levelled at people in high places, especially the church, I should probably cite the most significant book of the later Middle Ages or early Renaissance periods, *The Divine Comedy* of Dante Alighieri. Despite his liberalism, Dante still apparently accepted the old idea of the cosmos. His work is a trip through heaven, hell, and purgatory guided by the Roman poet Virgil. Along the way he places the world leaders of the time in their "proper" spots. Two popes, Boniface VIII and Celestine V, were placed in lower regions of burning sulpher or brimstone and lesser rogues were put in spots reserved for simpletons. A modern Dante would surely find room in such spots for some of the leaders responsible for the corrupt actions discussed previously.

Years ago I spent several years teaching in a foreign area with other Americans. In such a situation a genuine feeling of brotherly friendship developed. Possibly this is because "home" was far distant and the other culture was different. At any rate the "foreign" group often resorts to common picnics, dinners, golfing, and card parties. In such a situation a very closer friendship was developed between two families. Gradually one of the husbands because of envy became almost unbearable to his friends. I should mention that the offending member was the most "Christian" person of the whole faculty because he never missed Sunday church, sang in the choir, and taught Sunday school. Finally, I engaged this man in a heart to heart appeal to his conscience to salvage the friendship. His answer was "I have developed a philosophy of having no close friends." He had accepted the warmth and benefits of friendship—and had truly benefited—but couldn't accept or face his mutual responsibility. Taking communion for him was as effective, in my opinion, as drinking orange juice for breakfast. In my forty years of teaching in different schools at various levels, I have met many people of the above nature.

Moreover, on one of my hunting trips in the West, a guide told me the story of a man who tried to steal a patch of his neighbor's land by removing the official survey stakes. This was done so he would have parking place for cars without ruining his own lawn.[12a]

Throughout my adult life I have attended several funerals and in the services for people of this type it doesn't matter that they sinned along the way because at burial time they are assured an "elect" place if they have possessed the "proper" faith. Is this a needless cop-out of Christianity? At any rate, it seems that true faith should be more than "brief faith that fades under pressure"[13] or shows up just before death.

Some time ago a leading statesman and educator wrote to the effect that, hourly on campuses, in businesses and in government offices, men compromise their principles for promotion, money, and personal preferment. In my long years of teaching I have found this to be true and there is little difference between secular and church affiliated schools. It does appear that the church must do better in sermon, prayer, action. For example, according to numerous articles in the press, the faults of the churches do much to explain such mental aberrations as the Jim Jones tragedy, Scientology and possibly of something worse. What is frightening is that these "good" people help elect the leaders who might push the button to cause a nuclear castastrophe.

Therefore it is expeditious to continue our search for something relevant. However, when one surveys the current malaise of world society one is tempted to agree with Freud that research into anthropology and religion reduces religion to the status of a neurosis. In his opinion this explains its grandiose power.[14] And the church has had, does, and will have great power. Therefore in the West, every effort must be made to make it conform to the kernels of Christology. Of all the articles and books I have surveyed, the best promise seems to come from the works of Ludvig Andreas Feuerback. After being disgruntled with the hypocrisy of political and religious life in Germany, he secluded himself in a rural environment. In one of his sermons, for example, Feuerback proclaimed his refusal to be led by an animal worship dominated by "clerical donkeys and sheep," and "political wolves and tigers."[15] After much research and soul searching, he came up with some challenging suggestions. In his opinion theology was really anthropology. Ancient men worshipped things useful, powerful and usually what he didn't understand. The most universal object of worship was the sun because it is the source of all life and energy. But other items of power or utility were also idolized: the sea, animals, the wind, the rain. In a very definite sense, to the ancients to be "God" meant "to be useful." Possibly that may be the source of modern man's frustration. Next to the sun, the greatest source of power is nuclear energy. Its helpful uses are great but its dangers are frightening. It is hardly an object of worship.

God according to such thinking is nothing but the deified essence of man. History of religion, or what amounts to the same thing, the history of God, is as varied as mankind. "Just like the pagan gods, the Christian God originated in man. If he differs from pagan gods it is only because Christian man is different from pagan man."[16] This is much the same as what Pico della Mirandola said during the period of the Renaissance in his *Oration on Human Dignity*. That is, man differs from animals because he possesses a mind—let him use it and fly close to the Gods.[17] In that spirit let us turn to the next topic, Liberation Theology, and see what it has to offer.

V

Liberation Theology Plus

Inasmuch as a rather new movement among church leaders in Latin America is termed liberation theology and tends to place great stress on actually preforming or *doing* Christianity in a meaningful manner, this has been our concern in every chapter of this work. Anyone who believes in the diamonds or kernels of truth which are included in Christology must accept the general thrust of this movement as being very significant; not only for Latin America but the whole world.

However, one might accept the purpose and goals of this religious revolution but still criticize certain aspects. It was unfortunate, in this writer's opinion, that some of the exponents of this movement have based their claim for change on Exodus. For example, Dussel quotes God as saying, "I . . . have heard their cry of complaint against their slave drivers"[1] Therefore, liberate or "let my people go." But if one chooses to cite one part of the Bible story it is difficult to ignore the other aspects of the same book or chapter. In the whole story of Jehovah's treatment of the Egyptians, God is revealed as being a local god—narrowminded, violent, and bloodthirsty. It is moreover difficult for a historian to accept the story of Moses and the Exodus as other than a pious myth. Furthermore the emphasis on "my people" has caused other leaders of "tribes" to consider themselves "chosen," as I have indicated in previous chapters. This has led to much suffering and death.

Jehovah's killing of all the firstborn of Egypt and the ten

plagues are not exactly a good example for the handling of modern day problems. For example, Jehovah is revealed as not only cruel but jealous, arrogant, and spiteful. "What stories you can tell your children and grandchildren about the incredible things I am doing in Egypt! Tell them what fools I have made of the Egyptians and how I have proved I am Jehovah."[2] This is hardly the statement of a God that loves all men and is not a good precedent for the way to alleviate abuses that plague the world today in Africa, Latin America, and the Middle East.

It would be more appropriate to ground or find a basis for liberation theology in concepts which stem from the life and teachings of Christ. The story of Camilo Torres is relevant. Born of wealthy and aristocratic stock he dedicated himself to the priesthood to alleviate the crushing burdens of "the least of these." He felt he was chosen by Christ to be a priest and when his regular church efforts were opposed by the "establishment" of Christendom, he felt called upon to become a guerrilla revolutionary "because I am a priest." In his view the hierarchy of priorities in a truly Christian church should be reversed; that is, love, teaching of doctrine and last, formal worship.[3] In a little town of El Carmen, Colombia, he was ambushed and killed Febuary 15, 1966, because he opposed the interest of the establishment. The main theme of Christology seems to be love for the "least of these" but not just one's family, tribe, or the "chosen" few, but the people of the world. In like manner, the writers on liberation theology stress that love is a category of the Kingdom of God and inextricably interwoven with hope, mercy, and justice. In the opinion of these writers, histories of most existing churches are not universal at all but rather an account of religion as one aspect of national culture of Christendom, largely used by those in control to manipulate the political, social, and economic status quo; in other words, cultural imperialism.[4] It is love that Christ demonstrates in his struggle with the establishment in Jerusalem and for all men, Jews and gentiles alike. Therefore it seems unnecessary for the liberationists to resort to the rather primitive Old Testament to justify their movement. However, even the New Testament is apparently subject to enlightened interpretation. In the day-to-day preaching and application of the gospel to current problems, one must therefore agree with Hans Küng, who points out that there should be more openness in the church and that it has not been the Christian churches, even the reformation, that have brought about change, but rather men of the "Enlightenment." As a sign of hope, this influence stretches all the way from a Renaissance humanists such as Petrarch to Mahatma Gandhi, Pope John XXIII, Martin Luther King and the liberation theologians.[5]

Maybe we should emphasize again and again that liberation theology lays great stress on day-to-day searching for the meaning of current history in juxtaposition to Christology or the true Christian faith. Current events in the long span of history might include the happenings of a century or so. Some things in this recent period will be treated in a general manner, some more specifically.[6]

Obviously all of Latin America has been exploited. First by Portugal and Spain, largely for the precious metals, gold and silver. This might be termed the "old colonialism" of Christendom. After the political break from Spain in the nineteenth century, the new countries were subject to outside control from countries like Great Britain, Germany, France, and the United States. And despite the Monroe Doctrine (1823), by which the United States promised not to interfere in the internal affairs of the new budding "republics" and to protect them from the power-hungry empires of Europe, we shall term this period of Christendom, Neo-Colonialism. To stress the truth of the above statement as well as the duration of the period one might quote a statement of Mary Baker Eddy (founder of the Christian Science Church) carried in large type in the *New York Times* on the one hundredth anniversary of the doctrine: "I believe strictly in the Monroe Doctrine, in our Constitution, and in the laws of God."[7] Despite Mary Baker Eddy's belief in God and the promise we made in the doctrine itself not to interfere with existing colonies or dependencies, we have since acquired much that was Mexico (1848), "freed" Cuba, "acquired" Puerto Rico, and stolen the Panama Canal from Colombia. As I have already indicated, we have also interfered in many independent countries because of United States business investments in copper, tin, oil, bananas, as well as other interests—all done under the aegis of the Monroe Doctrine. In fact, one Latin American critic termed that instrument not a "doctrine but a dogma—and not a dogma but two, to wit; the dogma of the infallibility of the American presidents and the dogma of the 'Immaculate Conception' of the American foreign policy."[8]

We don't hear the Monroe Doctrine cited by the United States State Department often now. Possibly this is due to our violation of another precept found therein: "In the wars of the European powers in matters relating to themselves we have never taken any part, nor does it comport with our policy to do so."[9]

Mexico, Colonial

There are twenty-odd countries south of the Rio Grande including Brazil which have been subject to the two types of colonialism described above. To illustrate the problem the world faces between the have and have-nots or underdeveloped areas, it is not necessary to treat all or even a major number of these countries. Therefore, as in the case of Christendom, Mexico will be treated rather thoroughly and incidents in other states will be cited.

Relative to the early colonial years we have already commented on the enlightened thinking of churchmen such as Montesinos, Las Casas, and Bishop Juan de Zummáraga of Mexico.[10] In a sense they were the forerunners of the liberationists, but little progress was made, as writer Octavio Paz has pointed out in his *Labyrinth of Solitude*.

When the time came to break away from Spain, the Mexican version was quite different from the other areas with the exception of Haiti. By and large the lower classes, Indian and *mestizo*, had little understanding of the purpose of the revolution. In countries such as Argentina, Chile, Venezuela, and Peru the movement for independence was largely in the hands of the Creole class (native born people of Spanish ancestry). In Mexico the revolution, although led by a Creole, started out as a class war. Inasmuch as the colonies were obviously exploited there were sufficient grounds for revolution, especially after ideas began to seep into Latin America from the European "enlightenment."

The spark that really caused the break was Napoleon's

overthrow of the Spanish monarch Charles IV and his son Ferdinand. This caused *juntas*, local councils, to be set up that ruled in the name of Ferdinand VII. In Mexico after 1808 there was so much jockeying for power between the viceroy, council, and the *audiencia* that confusion resulted. This gave a Creole priest, Father Hidalgo, a chance to arouse the Indians in what amounted to a race war for freedom and independence. This finally started at Dolores with the cry of "long live our Lady of Guadalupe," their patron saint. At first the frenzied troops were successful, and with about 100,000 followers, Hidalgo marched toward Mexico City. However, he failed to strike before the conservative forces organized and was finally defeated and his forces annihilated at Calderón near Guadalajara in 1811. The patriotic leaders were, of course, captured and executed.

The next ten years were marked by much fighting between the conservative forces for power and involved the *peninsularies* (Spanish-born creoles) and some liberal revolutionary leaders—José Maria Morelos for example. By 1821 Augustin de Iturbide had gained control, and was crowned emperor on July 25, 1822. The empire was short lived, however. Antonio Lopez de Santa Anna was ambitious and issued a *pronounciamiento* or plan for the overthrow of Iturbide, which was accomplished. As a result Mexico became a "republic" in 1823 with the conservative element of society in power and the Roman Catholic Church recognized. This very brief account of the revolution in Mexico is given merely to emphasize that for Mexico—as well as elsewhere in Latin America after 1800—true revolutions did not materialize.[11] The Spanish rule was ousted, but the wealthy Creole element replaced the *peninsulares* and in cooperation with the powerful church, "the colonial period lived on."

Santa Anna

For thirty years the chameleon dictator, Santa Anna, dominated the scene in Mexico. It was a period of constant confusion, corruption, and continuous war. Santa Anna did not hold the presidency all the time but, behind the scenes, he usually was *jefe*, top boss. The chief issues were liberalism versus conservatism, federalism versus unitarianism, and landowners versus the landless. Add to this the ever-present *caudillo* (self-proclaimed military man) and one can understand why this period had many executives and many changes in the "form" of government.

In 1836 Mexico lost Texas despite Santa Anna's victory at the Alamo and massacre of the America troops. Some 166 defenders were exterminated. Later Sam Houston, the "big drunk" and ex-governor of Tennessee, captured Santa Anna in his underwear and Texas achieved independence as a result.

In 1845 Texas was annexed to the United States and friction over boundaries and other factors brought on the United States-Mexican War in which the latter country lost about a million square miles to the United States, including California and what became Arizona, New Mexico, Colorado, Utah, and Nevada.

From time to time a reformer would appear and attempt reforms, i.e., better justice, better schools, and other changes. Santa Anna's tactics as well as the clerico-military influence usually thwarted such efforts, and Mexico reached the 1850s in a sad state of affairs.

La Reforma

Briefly, this period lasted from 1854 to the French interlude, or until Porfirio Díaz took over in 1877. The hero in this period is Benito Juárez; the theme is reform directed mainly at the monopolistic landowners and clerical influence in cooperation with the army or *caudillo*. Laws were passed directed at curbing the influence of these groups, but naturally the privileged classes fought back. Juárez was excommunicated and the War of Reform (1858–1861) ensued. Juárez and his supporters won the war, but the reforms were not lasting. Probably the principal gain was the fact that Juárez became president in 1861. He arrived from Vera Cruz to little fanfare. He rode to the plaza, not in scarlet and gold and braided uniform, but in a black carriage, dressed in black clothes.[12] For the first time Mexico had a civilian ruler and reform had been directed at the power of the church, military, and land owners.

Porfirio Díaz

For our story, the period of French interlude of Maximilian I is of little significance. Napoleon III of France, wishing to bolster his popularity, was persuaded by Mexican conservatives that Mexicans would welcome liberation from the liberal regime of Juárez and his followers. Thus a scion of a European royal family was sent to take over Mexico. At first he was welcomed by some, but his extravagant expense account "wine bill" caused his popularity to soon fade and Juárez again won the battles. Maximilian was shot on the Hill of Bells near Querétaro, May 1867.[13] Juárez returned to the capitol in black carriage and black coat, the idea of monarchy now dead, Liberalism winning again.

We might dispense with a detailed discussion of the elections that followed. They were confusing. By 1877 Díaz had become constitutional president and dictator—a *caudillo* par excellence. The previous half century had been characterized by friction between the various segments of society, war, and little progress. Inasmuch as one of our main topics is liberation theology we might add that during this period the church cannot be blamed for all that was wrong, but can take little or no praise for promoting any significant reforms. And, it did excommunicate the greatest reformer of the period, Benito Juárez. I believe it was Victor Hugo who said the Western Hemisphere had produced three great men: Abraham Lincoln, Toussaint L' Ouverture (founder of the Republic of Haiti), and Benito Juárez—one a white man, one a black, and one an Indian.

Into this state of affairs stepped Porfirio Díaz and provided what Mexico probably needed most—stability. As indicated he was a powerful *caudillo* himself and he organized a very efficient national police force called the *rurales* who usually, in cases of uprising, shot first and asked questions afterward. Politically the policy of *pan o palo* (bread or a beating) was used effectively. In fact Mexico as seen from the outside was so calm it received praise from men such as Andrew Carnegie, Theodore Roosevelt, and Elihu Root as well as the German kaiser. Tolstoy even characterized Díaz as a "modern Cromwell." Nevertheless the dispossed masses, especially Indians, were abused and often treated as slaves. Díaz lacked the foresight and spirit to give *soul* to his work. Except for his native city, there are no national monuments in his honor.[14]

It is easy to understand why the foreigners viewed Mexico in such a rapturous manner, as one of the safest places in the world. Progress was made in the areas of transportation (railroads), irrigation, and the development of new land. But much of the profit went to foreigners. If all the property value had been added up in 1911 and divided, undoubtedly about 50 percent would have been owned north of the Rio Grande, hence the nickname for Díaz, "Mother of the Foreigners."

In the area of strictly social reform the record of Díaz is not so praiseworthy. The church regained some of the privileges lost during the period of *La Reforma*. Furthermore, little was done to promote education, especially for the lower classes. However, one important change did materialize: a middle class began to make its appearance. It almost seems that what happened under Díaz and after is typical of the frustration that exists in underdeveloped countries, especially Latin American. Confusion is followed by the stability of a strong dictatorship which is usually marked by privilege and corruption. Nevertheless, some benefits trickle down to the people and change and progress result.

Madero

Díaz "reigned" from 1877 to 1911, but by that time a liberal visionary, Francisco I. Madero, garnered enough support to overthrow the Díaz regime. However, Madero, a little man (slightly over five feet tall) with a brown beard, nervous tic, and high-pitched voice, was not the right person to control the disgruntled generals who hungered for power. Furthermore, the foreign interests, especially oil, didn't wish to see their privileges vanish because of such a reformer. Finally, United States Ambassador Henry Lane Wilson convinced Madero that Madero should resign. Victoriano Huerta, a man of dubious or even sinister qualities, became the "savior of Mexico" in the opinion of Ambassador Wilson.[15]

Apparently Madero and his vice president were promised safe exit through Vera Cruz. It is unfortunate indeed that on the way from one prison to another they were assassinated, undoubtedly under orders from Huerta. The excuse was *ley de fugo* (while attempting flight). Insofar as Ambassador Wilson was responsible for the resignation of Madero, he should also be held responsible for the results.[16]

Revolution

The assassination of Madero was followed by a pointless revolution and much suffering, the principal leaders being Emiliano Zapata, Venustiano Carranza, and Pancho Villa. The futility and frustration of the participants are pointed up by Mariano Azuelo in *The Underdogs*. We have the favorite wench of one fighting group stating her philosophy: "What damn fools—Where the hell do soldiers come from? . . . What the hell is the use of a revolution? Who's it for? . . . the folks who live in towns? Damn these rich people, they lock up everything."[17]

Insofar as this chapter is concerned primarily with theology and liberation, it is pertinent to end this part of the Mexican story with some of the significant changes wrought by the Mexican Constitution of 1917. At Querétaro the principal leaders of the revolution met in 1917 along with many enlightened humanists to solidify gains which had been envisioned ever since *La Reforma*. In books like *The Children of Sanchez* by Oscar Lewis, we learn that many of the clergy were human and not infallible. Moreover, it was almost axiomatic that the institution of the church as a whole was reactionary and in the past had usually been opposed to reform.

The old constitution had curbed the church schools to some extent. The new went even farther. Article III provided that all primary education must be secular. No church schools were permitted at lower levels. Article 27 confirmed national ownership of church lands. Article 30 was a catchall, curbing religious activities in general. For example, no religious political parties were to be allowed. Lastly, Article 23 provided for legislation to protect workers and bring about general welfare reforms.[18] This constitution has been dubbed "Mexico for Mexicans." It did not solve all the problems immediately. Little, for example, was done during the presidency of Carranza, who won out over the other revolutionary leaders. He was really rather conservative and when he failed to manipulate conditions so he could be re-elected, he filled a train with sacks of bullion from the treasury and fled to the coast. In the mountains on his way to Vera Cruz, his train was trapped and he was murdered in 1920.

For our purpose it is not necessary to survey in detail the administrations of Alvaro Obregón and Plutarco Elías Calles. Suffice to say that significant reforms were made in accordance with the Constitution of 1917 in areas such as agriculture, labor, education, and general culture, but they were minimal. For the sake of the main theme, the friction between church and state during Calles' last years should be noted because it reveals the type of church thinking that makes liberation theology almost impossible without violence. It also makes it easier to understand why enlightened individuals often criticize the establishment, which usually includes the church in Christendom, because it often helps repress the kind of thinking that leads to reform and enlightenment. The church at this time (1926) had called a strike against the government because it was carrying out the dictates of the Constitution of 1917, especially as to influence of clergymen in politics and education. Moreover, the Archbishop of Jalisco issued a pastoral letter which might be characterized as Middle Ages scholastic thinking.[19] (See p. 14.)

It should be clear to all that have had any education that this type of Middle Ages scholastic thinking has no place in "modern man's" world. Why, for example, suffer a hell on Earth for the prophetic paradise to come? Better to take Omar Khayyam's advice and "take the cash, and let the promised credit go." Better yet, use one's God-given mind to bring about sensible reform.

All features of the Mexican Revolution and Constitution have not been achieved, but Mexico seems to be on its way. A few years ago (1972) I visited Cocoyoc, a spa near Cuernavaca. There were gardens and flowers, a luxurous elevated eating place, and about six or seven swimming pools. Surprisingly, it was built not for the elite but apparently for the middle class—now maybe including anyone with money enough to pay the low rates. Such a development would have been impossible back in the days of the "progress" of Díaz. Truly Mexico has a right to consider itself an example and the leader of third-world countries.

Although Calles tried to perpetuate his control by choosing candidates who could carry out his wishes, Calles' authority had degenerated somewhat and a rift had developed between his followers and the National Revolutionary Party. Calles and his friends were sometimes termed the "millionaire socialists." or "forty thieves." After several bad choices for a puppet president Calles finally picked Lázaro Cárdenas who turned out to be the wrong man from Calles' point of view, but right for the Mexican people. Significant reform occurred, as we shall point out in the conclusion, as one example of reform in accord with the liberationists.[20]

Nature of Social Change

It has always puzzled me why it takes so long for enlightened men—theologians, philosophers, historians, and statesmen—to see the need for action in achieving proper reform. A case in point is the poignant story *Broad and Alien Is the World,* which describes an idyllic haven for life in a back-country village of Peru as it existed in the last century. Here the people had their common fields of wheat and corn as well as smaller private patches of vegetables. They were happy people. But from outside came power, money, clever businessmen, and lawyers who saw possibilities in their fields. Gradually, under the aegis of legal paper, and the concept of private property, they were exploited, robbed, and sometimes punished and killed. In short, money, power, and clever law-and-order men managed to steal the land and reduce the people to a state of peonage and slavery. They had lived, loved, and were happy, but after much fighting had to give up to what might be called "cultural imperialism." One sentence in the book is especially pertinent: "The Indian [was a] Christ nailed to the cross. Oh that damned cross!" This story is typical of the treatment of many of the have-not people in the underdeveloped areas of the world throughout the last four or five centuries, hence the title *Broad and Alien Is the World.*[21]

This is a classic story of problems that have plagued the "least of these" in all underdeveloped areas. Although liberation theology has received its greatest emphasis and thrust from theologians and guerrilla fighters in Latin America, it applies to the abused in all the world—even the Chicano grapefield workers of the industrialized state of California, followers of Cesar Chavez.

Other Ideas and Other Countries

It is not necessary to write specifically on all the twenty-odd republics of Latin America. The story above indicates the earlier picture of cultural imperialism. Now let us cite figures relative to standards of living that apply to the twentieth century. My own book on revolution cites such figures relative to the poverty spots of Latin America, but was based on rather old figures. However, these and others cited are viable because the proportions remain very much the same:

> To earn a loaf of bread a laborer worked 80 minutes in Colombia, 52 in Brazil, 69 in Guatemala and only 4.4 in the United States. Average per capita money income was about $275 in Latin America in the 1860s but over $2,000 [more now due to inflation] in the United States. One physician cared for the sickness and injury of 10,000 in Haiti whereas 13 served the same capacity in the United States. The same discrepancies can be noted regarding all factors related to the good life.[22]

However, it should be remembered that Mexico has made considerable progress since 1940.

Eduardo Frei Montalva cites land ownership figures:

> In Guatemala 0.51% of the farms cover 47% of the total arable land. In Ecuador 0.7% of landowners possess 37%. In Brazil 1.6% of the owners control over half the arable land and in Bolivia, before 1953, 6% of property owners

possessed 92%. In Cuba before the land reform, called for by the Constitution of 1940, only 1% of all farms accounted for 36% of the total area. Moreover, sugar plantations already in control of one half of the land extended their control to another 25% by rental leases.[23]

The same kind of analysis could be done for all the general factors of the "good life" such as housing, nutrition, and education. As Dussel states, a temporal dialetic is necessary on the priorities of Christianity. A true *dia logos* on the current historical situations in these have-not countries should result in comprehension from the old horizon to the present. Moreover, love and compassion must be put before formal lituragy and worship.[24]

What then is Christ? This question was asked of a young group from a Protestant church in Uruguay. The answer shot back immediately was "Jesus Christ is Ché Guevara."[25] What is startling is that a group of Christians should name a guerrilla fighter in this manner. Guevera was born of an aristocratic family and dedicated his life to helping "the least of these." After helping Castro in Cuba, he was killed in Bolivia as I have indicated.[26] Regarding this question, it should be noticed that the answer was not that Ché Guevara is Christ but rather Guevara that is Christ-like. Apparently others are beginning to think much the same thing. In one of the better recent books, Hans Küng observed that Ché Guevara, the Cuban guerrilla, bore a remarkable resemblance to the typical picture of Christ. In his opinion it did not seem surprising that Jesus had exercised a great influence on the revolutionary fighters such as Ché Guevara and Camilo Torres: "The Gospels presents us with an obviously clear-sighted, resolute, unswerving—if necessary also pugnacious and aggressive—Jesus." Moreover, he was not afraid of great distress, swords and danger and even death.[27] Hans Küng in discussing the difference between truth in science and religion quotes Carl Friedrick Von Weizsächer thus: "The present bourgeois status of the church is no proof that men are asking about Christian truth, this will be convincing when it is lived."[28] Many others have written much on these topics including Kierkegaard and Feuerback who wrote marvelously about "Christian love."[29] Feuerback even maintained that Luther was a bit of a humanist when it came to the goodness of God. He quotes Luther on Deuteronomy to this effect: "Thus reason describes God as what is helpful, useful, and beneficial to man." According to Luther this was true of the pagans, the Romans, the God of the papacy as well—"In the Scriptures the true God is called a *helper in affliction and the bestower of all good.*"[30]

We seem to have neglected Brazil and especially northeast Brazil where suffering, poverty, and suppression of human rights have possibly been as bad as any place in South America. As Bonino points out 41.6 percent of the total Brazilian industry is in foreign hands, 94 percent of the chemical, and all of the automotive. The naked truth is that "Brazil has become, not even a colony of foreign power, but a factory of multinational corporations; the Brazilian population, a reserve of cheap labor; and the Brazilian government, army, and police, foremen and wardens of these corporations."[31]

Here members of the church have played a dominant role as the address of Dom Helder Camara indicates. A prophetic statement much like that which Montesinos directed against old colonialism:

> I am a native of northeast Brazil, speaking to other natives of that region, with my gaze focused on Brazil, Latin America, and the world. I speak as a human being, in fellowship with the frailty and sinfulness of all other human beings; as a Christian to other Christians, but with a heart open to all individuals, peoples, and ideologies; as a bishop of the Catholic Church who, like Christ, seeks to serve rather than be served. May my fraternal greeting be heard by all: Catholics and non-Catholics, believers and nonbelievers. Praised be Jesus Christ![32]

It might now be the appropriate place to ask: Was Castro Christlike in his breaking away from the neocolonialism of the United States? Before we do this we should like to bring to your attention two pertinent concepts from Walter Lippman and Alfred North Whitehead to the effect that foreign policy should be decided by thought; reasonable, disinterested, and benevolent. And where knowledge is attainable and actions could be changed, wrong action has the taint of vice or possibly even sin.[33]

Cuba to the Bay of Pigs

We have already indicated how Cuba was acquired as a result of media propaganda in the United States and a president's prayer. To the war declaration was tacked the Teller Resolution which promised independence to the island. Undoubtedly this was salve to the collective conscience of the United States because after the Peace of Paris (1898) and the ousting of the Spanish, the United States began to act as though Cuba was conquered property. Incidentally, the Cubans who did most of the fighting for their independence were not allowed to take part in the peace conference, which is understandable when we consider the Platt Amendment. Before the now "free" Cubans were allowed to draw up their own constitution, they were forced to accept the above amendment which allowed the United States possession of certain strategic sites in Cuba (including Guantánamo Bay), prohibited the Cubans from making foreign loans which might threaten their "independence," and allowed the United States to interfere when necessary.[34] Thus Cuba was really a colony until the abrogation of the Platt Amendment in 1934.

During this period and even after 1934, the United States Ambassador undoubtedly had more influence than the Cuban president. On one occasion a Cuban president was being praised for the close friendship with the United States Ambassador. His answer was in essence: "Yes, but I wish he wouldn't be so public about it."

There were leaders who seemed genuinely interested in real reforms and in helping the *campesino* or forgotten man. This was true of both Machada and Batista. But it must be remembered that Americans, before Castro's time, owned 80 percent of the utilities, 90 percent of mines and cattle ranches, and almost all of oil refining as well as large interests and influence in railways, the sugar industry, and banks. These owners were interested primarily in profit and the presidents were often subject to under-the-table deals. Not surprisingly, the presidents often built luxurious homes on meager salaries and Batista, when ousted by Castro, retired wealthy and even settled a small fortune on his estranged wife.[35]

In 1940 Cuba adopted a new constitution quite similar to the 1917 constitution of Mexico. Like Carranza, Batista didn't enforce it, and this accounts for the revolutionary activity of Castro. First imprisoned but allowed freedom, Castro's "history will absolve" speech made it plain he meant to make Cuba really free. Despite abrogation of the Platt Amendment, Cuba was still "ours to lose" and naturally the United States government and all investment people were concerned. Castro had a Robin Hood image and he didn't have to become—and probably wasn't—a communist because all he had to do was enforce the Constitution of 1940. That would be doing much for the lower classes. What irked the United States was not so much communism but the fact that a "pipsqueak" had the temerity to think he could free Cuba. Nevertheless, with great audacity he won out over Batista and started a new era—possibly for all third world countries. After Batista fled and Castro gained control, coming in from the Sierra Maestra, there was danger of a bloody massacre such as occurred after Machado was ousted in the early 1930s. To prevent this Castro held public trials; no good historian would deny that most of those killed were guilty. Immediately criticism arose in the United States over such bloody tactics. Previously many more had been killed cruelly and without public trial. No protest was made then. One priest witnessed the Batista period: "To people who had had their fingernails ripped off, their eyes gouged out . . . [and] who had seen their sons, fathers, and husbands tortured, the public trials and punishments were just retribution for what Batista and supporters had perpetrated."[36] Apparently America had forgotten 1775 and 1776 which saw written the words: *Mantenemos estas verdades como evidentes: que todos hombres son creados eguales* . . . We hold these truths to be self evident, that all men are created equal.

After this, affairs between Cuba and the United States went from bad to worse. Diplomatic embassies were mutually withdrawn. Castro proclaimed himself a communist and that he would always remain one. And the United States began to operate from secret bases in Guatemala, islands in the Caribbean, and Florida to attack and overthrow Castro as it tried in the Bay of Pigs fiasco. This was of course contrary to the United Nations as well as Article 15 of the Organization of American States because at that time Castro was probably supported by over 80 percent of the Cubans. Because our past image was often thought of as being pure in accordance with the Judeo-Christian precepts, this comment is relevant: "The trouble was that we were acting like an old whore and trying to pretend . . . the sweet young thing we used to be."[37]

Probably the story could have been different. As it was in Mexico, and as we shall relate in the conclusion, if the United States State Department and the president had followed the advice of Philip Bonsal who wanted to follow the policy of waiting, caution, and understanding as Josephus Daniels did in the oil dispute in Mexico. From here on conditions worsened and the world had a terrifying scare in the form of the missile crisis of 1962. So the time has come to abandon the un-American, un-Christian and anti-humane doctrine that what is ultimate in international relations and the shaping of history is physical power, material wealth, and the relentless spirit of self-interest.[38] Humanity tottered on the brink of nuclear war; by the skin of our teeth disaster was avoided.

Conclusion

During the writing of this book, the author has conducted a poll. Many people have been asked directly and indirectly what one must do to survive. As Herbert Marcuse points out in his *One-Dimensional Man*, one reason seems to be too many gadgets and conveniences which satisfy us in too affluent a manner and yet cause frustration. But probably what worries most is the possibility of a nuclear disaster—war related or otherwise.[39]

But there are hopeful things to mention.

Sigmund Freud seems to have had the same idea a half century ago:

> The fateful question of the human species seems to me to be whether and to what extent the cultural process de-

veloped in it will succeed in mastering the derangements of communal life caused by the human instinct of aggression and self-destruction. In this connection . . . men have brought their powers of subduing the forces of nature to such a pitch that by using them they could now very easily exterminate one another to the last man. They know this—hence arises a great part of their current unrest, their dejection, their mood of apprehension. And now it may be expected that the other of the two "heavenly forces," eternal Eros, will put forth his strength so as to maintain himself alongside of his equally immortal adversary.[40]

In my early student days, James H. Breasted was considered one of the greatest of the ancient historians. In his book the *Dawn of Conscience* (Scribners, 1933) he points out that man has fashioned destructive weapons for possibly a million years whereas conscience and monotheism emerged as social forces only four to five thousand years ago. There appears to be hope.

Moreover, enlightened churchmen seem to be countering the "fundamentalist" element. Either the Christian Mission must come to the Muslem and the Hindu or they must come together in some way.[41]

And Hans Küng stresses that the followers of Buddha, Confucius, Lao-tse, Zarathustra, Mohammed and others are inspired by the same longing as true Christians. Küng is even ready to see some good in Marxism, especially his emphasis on the economic factor in history. Instead of the inhuman conditions which first resulted from the brutal features of the early Industrial Revolution, much social reform and change has resulted from Marxian thinking in the labor arena. Even the Russian people—despite the evils of the Lenin-Stalin period—owe Marx much because of humanistic socialism. The messianic communism of the Lenin-Stalin period which practices the domination of men over men is an imperialist policy worse than capitalism and is what must be avoided.[42]

Lest some readers take offense at even the mention of good that might derive from the thinking of Karl Marx, a few additional remarks might help clarify the problem. Many do not realize, for example, the mental poison that remains in the US from the long period of McCarthyism. This seems to be especially true when pride, the pocketbook, or politics are involved. It is difficult for many Americans to realize that many revolutions of a general welfare type—similar to what occurred in the thirteen colonies—are not necessarily associated with the dictates of the Kremlin, but are *sui generis*.

Earlier I mentioned a significant talk given by Felix Greene on China and the world situation.[43] Explaining the current break in friendly relations between China and the U.S.S.R. he used the well-known quote of Marx: "Christianity is the opiate of the masses." According to Greene, Marx also said religion can be the *soul* of a soulless world. Apparently he thought that China was capable of developing a better "soul" than the U.S.S.R.

One of the better recent books treating Marx not only points out many of his inconsistencies—for which he might be forgiven if one analyzes the thinking of current world leaders—but also notes many of the differences between the Lenin-Stalin dictatorship and the thinking of Marx and Friedrich Engels.

In 1842 Marx wrote: "A free press is the principal, reasonable moral essence of freedom. The character of a censored press is the unprincipled aberration of freedom, it is civilized abomination, a perfumed monster."[44] In his writings he also stressed that any form of government should be democratic, not a bureaucratic despotism. It is unfortunate indeed that he denied God, that is, the God of Christianity, because his thinking as it worked out in Russia created a religion and a "God," namely Lenin, for the politburo and the presidium.

One cannot deny some of the brutal aspects of the factory system created by the Industrial Revolution. By the same token, one must admit that Marx was concerned deeply with the welfare of "the least of these." This is why many of the liberation theologians can accept the economic doctrine of Marx and try to achieve it in accordance with Christology.[45]

Undoubtedly Marx envisioned a humanistic type of communism such as Tito created in Yugoslavia or what some countries are striving for in the have-not areas of the world—Africa, parts of Asia and Latin America. If Russia had been the home of Marx during and after 1917, he would undoubtedly have been sent to Siberia or spent his last years in exile. In actuality he spent his last years in democratic England.

Recently the *Lutheran Standard* carried several pertinent

statements concerning love and brotherhood. The first was a quote from St. Paul, "If I speak in the tongues of men . . . but have not love, I am a noisy gong or a clanging symbol." Relative to the hate engendered by the Tehran hostage crisis, Lila C. Clawson concludes that only in the context of brotherly love can our broken world community be restored.[46]

Probably the most heartening evidence of a change of attitude is found in one issue of the *Washington Spectator*. The first account is rather typical: Marie Ego and six friends were led into prison. As it turned out, Ego and her friends were nuns of the Sisters of Loretto, a socially active order with a chapter in Colorado. The seven women were handcuffed, chained, and imprisoned for protesting against nuclear weapons. Apparently they had trespassed on federal property at Rocky Flats near Denver. When questioned by the *Greeley* [Colorado] *Tribune*, Sister Ego stated: "In case of nuclear war 140 million Americans would be killed and 40 to 50 million more would die later of radiation."[47]

Another significant comment in this issue credits the church as the major force for change in Latin America. The United States National Conference of Catholic Bishops has supported church militants in Latin America and comments, "the landless peasants and the ministers of the Church" are on one side in El Salvador, and on the other are "the national security forces and the landed oligarchy."[48] This issue included at least a dozen examples of this type of concern and was entitled "The Church Militant and Social Action."

Inasmuch as this book will be read by people of the West who have functioned under capitalism and Christendom, one should end on a positive note—easily done in writing but not always carried out in practice.

As I have already stated regarding Mexico, Calles picked the wrong man as a puppet when he chose Lázaro Cárdenas. He was much like Castro although he knew that the backing of the National Revolutionary Party meant certain election. Still he canvassed the country thoroughly to assertain the real needs of the lower class.

During his presidency (1934–40), land distribution more than doubled. Although the policy of *minifundia* has turned out to be not all good, that is hindsight. Cárdenas kept his promise and his personal contact was good training in the problems of agriculture and social justice, and had psychological value. Other reforms were also forthcoming especially in the area of labor.

But the real problem developed with *El Coloso del Norte* (the United States) over wages to workers in the petroleum industry. The workers asked for higher wages and Cárdenas thought it was just. The oil companies protested, but to no avail. On March 18, 1938, Cárdenas nationalized the oil industries. Of course there was friction. The oil companies wanted at least a half billion dollars for their property. (They had already taken out huge profits.) Cárdenas protested and appointed a group to investigate, which angered the companies. Apparently the oil companies approached the U.S. Secretary of State and tried to get the United States government to manipulate the price of silver to hurt Mexican sales. The oilmen also requested that the ambassador, Josephus Daniels, be recalled.

Daniels was outwardly ill qualified for the task of ambassador. He was seventy years of age and spoke no Spanish, but he tried to look at problems from both sides. Soon he was dubbed *simpatico* by the Mexicans. He was also a friend of Franklin D. Roosevelt who advised him to "play possum"—remain in Mexico and settle the issue fairly. The oil companies finally got about $24,000,000—not half a billion. Today Mexico celebrates March 18, 1938 as its second day of independence.

David Cronon did a biography of Daniels and ends this episode with the statement: He was "a devout Methodist who had a deep and abiding faith in the efficacy of the Golden Rule."[49]

This settlement with Mexico is, in my opinion, one of the few times a grave question has been settled in accordance with spiritual and democratic principles. It has paid off. Today students attend many schools and institutes in Mexico, tourists go to Vera Cruz and Acapulco. More importantly, the presidents of the two countries have met periodically on or near the border to settle their mutual problems mutually—a good precedent. Let us hope for more settlements of this type. Although now rather late, possibly the Cuban situation could be adjusted in accord with the same precepts. We need right now a rousing *jon ron,* (home run) bases loaded, Latin American style, for Christology. Not only would it bring in more "ballplayers" from Cuba but the roar of applause would echo throughout the world.

When a *great* event such as the achievements of Daniels in Mexico occurs, why isn't it publicized with headlines and fanfare as was Admiral Dewey's victory over the Spanish at Manila Bay in 1898—or even the Super Bowl football game? Is this the fault of the home, schools, or the government? Possibly the story of Carlos Fuentes' treatment by our government in the 1960s is significant. An article he has written seems to indicate that he foresaw what was going to happen in spots like Cuba, Chile, Panama, and Mexico vis-à-vis the United States. Therefore he challenged our subsecretary for Latin American affairs to a debate. The necessary visa for travel to the United States was denied by Ambassador Mann. This, despite our emphasis on the "sacredness" of the free flow of ideas. Then Fuentes wrote an article in *Siempre (Always)* where he reviewed past policies of the United States and made some rather prophetic statements at the end of his article. For example, science could bring to *todos los hombres* (all men) despite differences in religious creed, sex, or race, freedom from sickness, ignorance, and hunger. Especially was this needed in the emerging third world or underdeveloped countries. But here he had a warning of the politicization which might develop between the United States and the Union of Soviet Socialist Republics as to aid and control of these areas. Cold war *could* yield to "*guerra caliente*" (hot war).[50] He challenged the ambassador to answer, but such was not forthcoming. Unfortunate indeed! Much money and energy might have been saved and spared. More importantly, in line with the proper precepts, brotherly love might have been advanced.

Fuentes went on to state that Mexico and the United States didn't have to be rivals. Mexico had much respect for American efficiency and the heritage that stems from the likes of Lincoln, Franklin D. Roosevelt, Poe, Melville, Faulkner, Marian Anderson and others.

In 1938 Fuentes was a student in the United States who praised Cárdenas for his nationalization of Mexican oil in 1938. For this he was insulted and turned on by fellow students who had liked him, because of the "crazy men" who ran his country.

Now Carolos Fuentes is apparently no longer a bad "socialist or communist" and has taught in universities and written articles in reputable United States' newspapers. In one such article from the *New York Times* news service. Fuentes pointed out that during President Carter's recent visit to Mexico, President Lopez Portillo was trying to say: "Please understand us as a civilization and not as a series of agreements about tomatoes." In view of the article's title "Iran seems like Mexico in 1915," Fuentes implies that Iran should be considered a civilization and not just a source of oil.[51]

The situation as indicated has been much better between the United States and Mexico than elsewhere. But if people with the knowledge available would have followed a rational course yesterday, then today's situation would be almost perfect. Who is to blame in this specific case, the government which refused admittance to Fuentes in 1962, or the people and institutions who elect the officers of the government who decide questions relative to Mexico, Cuba, Panama, Chile, or Iran?

Because of its recent oil discoveries, Mexico might emerge from its third world status to a "rookie" first rate power. Therefore a comment from Octavio Paz seems especially seminal and relevant. In his words:

> We [Mexicans] are no longer "Don No One." That status once protected but also oppressed us, hid us but also disfigured us. If we tear off the masks, if we open up ourselves, if, in brief, we face our own selves, then we can truly begin to live and think. Nakedness and defenselessness are awaiting us. But there in the open solitude transcendence is also waiting: The outstretched hands of other solitary beings. For the first time in our history, we are contemporaries of all mankind.[52]

The world is woven of many races—red, white, yellow, black and brown—which include various economic, political, and religious institutions. The fate of one has become the fate of all. This is not a prediction but a description of the present world. Let it so remain in love and understanding of one another.

Addendum: Educational Suggestions

International Level

1. The U.S. alone or through the United Nations should promote an "Oak Ridge" for the peaceful settlement of international problems.

Reason: In 1945—the dropping of the atomic bomb—I listened to a lecture at the University of Minnesota by a noted scientist. In this discourse it was stated that before World War II most scientists thought it would take several million years to develop nuclear power. At Oak Ridge, Tennessee, the U.S. brought together a "bank" of brains to improve expertise in killing and the bomb was developed in two years.

Wouldn't it be a blessing if the problems between nations could be settled in a more civilized manner—say for example the results of a soccer, basketball game, or even a Ping-Pong match?

2. The U.N. should appoint a committee to produce an objective course treating problems and problem areas of the world. This should be written by experts from all parts of the world. It should be requested that such courses be taught in all the countries represented in the U.N.

Reasons:

1. It has been said that history is a fairytale which most authorities accept—that is, within a nation. Obviously, all his-

tory is biased by such factors as nationalism, money, race, and religion. A course so constituted would be more objective.

2. For the same reason a course in comparative religions should also be so constructed and its contents be requested or required. In religion-affiliated schools it should be taught by an instructor of a different denomination of the school where taught. Possibly the federal or central government could withhold federal aid unless such a course were offered.

3. Furthermore, something very significant and of immediate concern should be done. This same U.N. committee could promote an international T.V. debate. *60 Minutes* with Mike Wallace, and Dan Rather, should be asked to present to a world audience a two-hour evaluation or critique of Russia's moves in parts of the world other than the U.S.S.R. and the possible violations of Helsinki or Salt agreements. Then Russia should be extended the same privilege. After this the Third World countries should be heard from with their representatives, of course. The U.N. should be allowed to check to ascertain that such a program is really brought to the people. In other words, the free flow of ideas should not be embargoed.

4. On June 28, 1914, a rather minor incident occurred at Sarajevo, the capital of Bosnia, a province which earlier Austria had wrestled from Serbia. Here Archduke Francis Ferdinand, heir presumptive of the Austrian throne, was assassinated. This climaxed a series of at least five crises—the Algeciras incident (1906) to the Balkan Wars 1912–13. After each of which the great powers flexed their fighting muscles by increasing the size of navies and armies until Europe was literally a big bristling hand grenade. As a result World War I ensued—the first holocaust of the twentieth century as indicated above.

Relative to these events and wars in general a concept which I acquired years ago might still be pertinent, to wit: If mankind is capable of learning any lessons from events which preceded WWI it should be clear that the way to achieve peace is not to promote crises and prepare for all-out war! As we have already indicated the results of a third World War are awesome to contemplate—and it is civilians who will suffer, as much or more than the military element. Therefore the common man should be informed. Moreover, if such a program can be promoted it should be *publicized*! If, on the other hand, the "other side" refuses in such a peace effort then the dissatisfied countries of the world should realize that the present situation is not honest and *realpolitik* must ensue!

University and College Level

1. The professor teaching the history and philosophy of education in the teacher training program should be a person well grounded in "education," psychology, religion, philosophy, and history—in short, a paragon of wisdom and a great teacher.

Reasons:

In the past I have taken such courses usually taught by someone poorly qualified and the end result is a boring offering which gives "education" a bad image.

Most of the national and world citizens who vote for the leaders who will decide seminal questions of the day are high-school educated. Even though some teachers specialize in such areas as language, home economics, and shop, they should be cognizant of the significant social problems of the day. The above course should provide such knowledge. Also, such a teacher should be paid more than the football coach, choir director, or even the deans.

2. It is questionable whether philosophy should be taught at religious affiliated colleges or universities.

Reason: All education is dedicated to a constant search for the truth. Most religious oriented schools support dogmas or doctrines of an absolute nature. Real philosophy does not thrive in such an atmosphere. If "philosophy" is taught in such schools, it should be renamed. Moreover there should be no "capstone" course dominated by the "philosophy" departments.

Lower Levels

1. Teachers or professors in the grades or high school should be as well qualified and paid as well as those in colleges or universities.

Reason: Biases are acquired early and it takes an excellent, well-qualified teacher to handle the untruths that derive from nationalism, religion, and racial price.

2. No religion should be allowed in the public schools; thus making it possible for religion to serve chauvinistic nationalism. It might be wise in church as well as parochial schools not to expose young people to serious religion until they have reached the age when rational thinking is possible.

Reason: Years ago when I read the biographical sketch of John Stuart Mill, one of the great thinkers of nineteenth century England, I noted that his father insisted that he should not be exposed to religion at an early age. Also, in my long years of teaching in America and abroad I have noted numerous cases where young people, through the clergy and usually the distaff side of the family, have absorbed creed, dogma or doctrine that then becomes the absolute "truth." This sometimes makes it difficult if not impossible to dispense real enlightened liberal arts education later.

Years ago I attended a conference of religion-affiliated colleges where it was pointed out that in a large metropolitan area an overall history of that church body was desired, but there were seven different denominations. The "historians" came up with seven different "histories." Such distortion obviously makes the search for truth difficult at all levels of instruction.

A former U.S. Ambassador to the United Nations congratulated the *Washington Spectator* for its publication a year earlier entitled "Leashing the Dogs of War." It would therefore be fitting to stress several significant concepts from this article. The article emphasizes the awesome consequences that have resulted from the new techniques of modern warfare, "agent orange" for example, and even from the tests of the nuclear proving grounds in the deserts of Nevada. Several statements are especially significant.

The situation seems so grim that a Swedish paper asked a well-known author, Kurt Vonnegut (*Slaughterhouse Five*), to give his imaginative view of World War III. His answer: "My mind refuses. Writing is a hopeful business. One cannot write about the end of hope."[1]

One concept is truly certain, each new step or weapon we build merely causes the Soviets to build more. This should cause us to ponder seriously the current art-of-war situation. Today's world history—as I have implied above—seems to be a race between meaningful education and catastrophe.

We might end with a concept taken from Tennyson's Ulysses and paraphrased: "Experience is an arch where thro' gleams the ever new world with new margins." This demands a doubting and questioning of the old myths and ideas and the courage to experiment with and fashion something new and better.

Notes

Chapter I

1. Hauberg, C. A. "It's Time for a Change: To World Peace and Security," *The Social Studies*. April 1945, pp. 143–145.

2. Hayes, Carlton J. H. *History of Europe*, Vol. II. Chapter XXIII. Macmillan & Co. May 1939. c. 1916.

3. This article was the result of research by an international panel submitted to the United Nations' Secretary General U. Thant. *The Saturday Review of Literature*. December 9, 1967.

4. *Ibid.*

5. *The New Republic*. October 20, 1979, pp. 15–17. In the past Clausewitz has been recognized as a world authority on the art of warfare by conventional methods.

6. Galbraith, John K. *The Affluent Society*. Houghton, Mifflin and Co., Boston. 1958, p. 5.

7. In 1633 Galileo was forced to recant his beliefs before the Inquisition. But it is rumored that after his recantation he muttered *Eppur si muove* (The earth does move). Stearns, Raymond P. *Pageant of Europe*, Harcourt Brace & Co., New York 1947. pp. 66–68.

8. Sikes, J. G. *Peter Abelard*. Russell & Russell Inc., New York, 1961, pp. 72, 83.

9. Phillips, J. B. *Appointment with God*. Macmillan Co., New York, 1954, p. v.

10. Felix Greene was billed at *Belles Artes* as one of the leading experts on modern China. His work includes a position in the office of the British prime minister, freelance writing, and considerable radio and TV exposure. The title of his last book is especially significant: *Let There Be a World* (Fulton, 1963).

11. Pollard, A. F. *Evolution of Parliament*. Chapter IX. Longmans Green & Co., London, 1920.

12. Carroll, Lewis. *Through the Looking-Glass*.

13. This writer has had occasion to converse with door-to-door disciples of this type of thinking who believe, apparently, that God has accounted for the petroleum deposits in the Middle East so that Armageddon would result.

See also, Goodman, Ellen: "A Chill Wind from the 'Creationists,' " *Minneapolis Tribune*, April 16, 1980, p. 8A.

14. Howes, Robert G. "Silence from the Churches." *Minneapolis Sunday Tribune*, August 12, 1979.

15. *Minneapolis Tribune*, August 9, 1979.

16. *The Washington Spectator*. Tristram Coffin, Ed. Washington, D.C. March 15, 1980.

17. *Ibid.*

18. During Batista's repressive period, thousands of the opposition lost their lives in very cruel ways—castration, slicing of breasts, for example. Little of such news was covered by the United States media or many of the historians. Later, even the esteemed Arthur Schlesinger, Jr., went along with the administration policies of John F. Kennedy, apparently because he valued "influence" more than professional integrity and morality, despite his earlier statements to the contrary. As reported in *Time* he was willing to lie if necessary: "Either you get out or you play the game." Hauberg, C. A., *Latin American Revolutions*. T. S. Denison & Co., Minneapolis, 1968, pp. 199 f.n., 243 f.n. *Time*. December 17, 1965, pp. 54–60.

19. *Washington Spectator* , March 15, 1980.

Chapter II

1. Pike, James. *A Time for Christian Candor*. Harper & Row. 1964. p. 31.

2. Edwards, David L. *Honest to God Debate*. Westminster Press. 1963. p. 35.

3. Robinson, John A. T. *Honest to God*. Westminister Press. Philidelphia. 1963. p. 141.

4. Edwards. *Honest to God Debate*. pp. 80–81.

5. Redmond, Howard A. *The Omnipotence of God*. Westminister Press. Philidelphia, Pa. 1952.

6. Ault, Warren. G. *Europe in the Middle Ages*. D. C. Heath & Co. New York. 1932. p. 408.

7. D'Antonio, William V. and Pike, Frederick B., Eds. *Religion Revolution and Reform: New Forces for Change in Latin America*. Prager. New York. 1964. p. 250.

8. Quoted in Hauberg, C. A. *Latin American Revolution*. T. S. Denison & Co. 1968. p. 40.

9. Niebuhr, Ursula, Ed. Harper & Row, New York. 1947. Frontispiece.

10. *Ibid.*

11. Christology and Christianity are often used synonomously. Christology is that branch of theology dealing with the original person and nature of Jesus Christ. Christianity would include this, but also the writing about Christ and the added interpretations.

12. According to Barbara W. Tuckman, the Black Death caused people to question the absolutes of the fixed order of society and God's role. Minds so opened are hard to shut and thus the Black Death "may have been the unrec-

ognized beginning of modern man." *A Distant Mirror.* Alfred Knopf. New York, 1978. p. 123.

13. See above p. 12.

14. All mentioned have been cited already except the latter which is really a comment on the challenge of Rudolf Bultman, Cairns, David. S.C.M. Press, LTD. London. 1960.

15. Pike, James. *Christian Candor.* p. 63.

16. Hoffer, Eric. *The True Believer: Thoughts on the Nature of Mass Movements.* Harper & Bros. New York. 1951. p. 35.

17. Robinson is sometimes listed as John A. T. and other times as just A.T. Robinson, which we shall use hereafter.

18. *Time.* November 11, 1966, "Religion." 56–58, 63–64.

19. See above p. 4.

20. Morrison, Samuel E. and Commager, Henry S. *The Growth of the American People.* Oxford Univ. Press. New York. 1942. p. 88; Hayes, Carlton. J. H. *History of Europe,* Vol. I. p. 88.

21. See above p. 4 and note 7.

22. Edwards. *Honest to God Debate.* pp. 49, 98.

23. Hoffer, Eric. *The True Believer.* p. 78.

24. Peter of course was one of the original twelve Apostles but Paul was not, however. He was known as the Apostle of the Gentiles.

25. Many Christians in the Middle East did not accept the idea of the Bishop of Rome being the "Vicar of Christ" and later the Greek Orthodox Church broke away from Roman dominance. MacKinney, Loren C. *The Medieval World.* Rinehart & Co., Inc. New York. 1947. p. 77.

26. Lunt. W.E. *History of England.* Harper & Bros. New York. 1938. p. 137.

27. Heaton, Herbert. *The Economic. History of Europe.* Harper & Bros. New York. 1936. p. 89.

28. *American Historical Review.* Vol. XVIII p. 1–12 (Paper read at A.H.A. Dec. 28, 1921.)

29. *Ibid.*

30. "Lay investiture" means the appointment of the clergy to office by the secular prince.

31. *Unam Sanctam* means there were two swords, one wielded by the pope spiritually and one by the prince secularly, but for the pope. Lucas, Henry S. *The Renaissance & the Reformation.* Harper & Bros. N.Y. 1934. p. 22.

32. *Ibid.*, p. 60–62. This event really anticipates what we shall call Christendom, that is, the growing tendency of the church to dominate the secular state. It had shown itself much earlier under such popes as Gregory the Great (590–604) and Gregory VII (1073–1086).

33. *Ibid.* pp. 435–437. The collection and disbursement of money by the popes illustrates well why there should be concern on the part of the reformers. During the reign of John XXII at Avignon a new method of tax collection was devised called the *collectoria.* Inasmuch as the middle class was replacing the feudal as a source of income a more effective system was needed. Seven different kinds of taxes were collected including the decima (tenth), annates or first fruits, and the right of spoils; 67.3 percent of this income was spent on war, and other political and secular needs almost exhaused the rest. Lucas. *Ibid.* pp. 73–75.

34. Ault. *Europe in the Middle Ages.* pp. 405–409.

35. Lucas. *Renaissance and Reformation* p. 242–244; Creighton, Mendel. *A History of the Papacy During the Period of the Reformation.* Vol. III. p. 75.

36. In the *Canterbury Tales* of Chaucer (c. 1343–1400) there is little that is complimentary to the church. The only person praised is the parson: "He wayted after no pomp or reverence. Ne maked him a spyced conscience. But Christes lore, and his apostles twelve, He taughte, and first he folwed it hemselve."

37. Stearns, Raymond O., *Pageant of Europe*, Harcourt Brace & Co., N.Y. 1947, p. 29.

38. John Addinton Symonds quoted in Stearns. *Ibid.* p. 5.

39. Taylor, H. O. *Thought and Expression of the 17th Century*, Macmillan & Co., New York, 1920, p. 281.

40. Hayes. *History of Europe* Vol I. p. 157.

41. In other words, the peasants and people generally were told to follow the ruling prince in religious matters. This constitutes the principle of divine right of kings.

42. J. A. Figgis as quoted in Lucas. *Renaissance and Reformation.* p. 417.

43. *Ibid.* p. 438.; *New Catholic Encyclopedia.* Editorial Staff of Catholic University. Washington, D.C. 1906. pp. 1085–1091.

44. *Ibid.* p. 438.

45. Lunt. *History of England.* p. 392.

Chapter III

1. *Saturday Evening Post.* December 1979. (Cover.)

2. Bonino, José. *Doing Theology in a Revolutionary Situation.* Fortress Press. Phil. 1975. Foreword xiv, xv.

3. "Moors" is the common name for the Moslems or followers of Mohammed who invaded Spain from Morocco.

4. Tarik has acquired lasting fame indeed because the huge rock he took is still called *Gebel-al-tarik* or hill Tarik, Gibraltar.

5. Ault. *Europe in the Middle Ages.* p. 313.

6. According to some authorities there was "grave doubt" whether Saint James the Apostle ever appeared in Spain. Diffie, B. W. *Latin American Civilization, Colonial Period.* Stackpole Sons. Harrisburg, Pa. 1945. p. 233.

7. The history of church-state relations is much the same for Portugal and Brazil except that the Portugueese were a bit more tolerant. A Portugueese has been described as a Spainard without the warlike flame or dramatic orthodoxy of the *conquistador* of Mexico and Peru.

8. Hauberg, C. H. "Cortes: Conquestador." *Current History.* March 1954. pp. 137–144.

9. Herring, Hubert. *A History of Latin America.* Alfred A. Knopf. New York. 1968. p. 171.

10. Dussel, Enrique. *History of the Theology of Liberation.* Mary Knoll, New York. Orbis Books. 1976. pp. 83–84.

11. Hange, Lewis. *Aristotle and the American Indians*. Indiana University Press. Bloomington. 1959. p. 24.

12. Diffie. *Latin American Civilization*. p. 255–56.

13. *Ibid.*, pp. 255–56.

14. Dussel. *Theology of Liberation*. p. 80.

15. Trevelyan, G. M. *Lord Grey and the Reform Bill*. London. 1920. p. 272ff.

16. Morison, Samuel E. & Commager, Henry S. *The Growth of the American Republic*. Oxford Univ. Press. New York. 1942. p. 330.

17. Pike. *Christian Candor*. pp. 51–52.

Chapter IV

1. Hart, Bernard. *The Psychology of Insanity*. Macmillan & Co. New York. 1937. pp. 139–140, 150.

2. Viscott, David S. M.D. *The Making of a Psychiatrist*. Arbor House, New York. 1972. p. 37.

3. *Ibid.* pp. 25, 88.

4. *Ibid.*, p. 20.

5. Quoted in Hart. *Psychology of Insanity*. p. 96.

6. Hereafter called the Shah.

7. *Minneapolis Star*. Dec. 5, 1979. Section A. pp. 1, 24.

8. Shah, Khalid. "The Myth of an Islamic Brotherhood." *Minneapolis Tribune*. Sunday June 8, 1980, section A, part 2, p. 13.

8a. U.S. covert action in Chile is fully substantiated by the Staff Report of the U.S. Senate Select Committee to Study Government Operations with respect to the CIA, i.e. *Covert Action in Chile*. U.S. Government Printing Office, Dec. 18, 1975.

9. In 1969 this writer was counselor for Minnesota SPAN (Student Project for Amity of Nations) in Bolivia. This resulted in interviews with Paz Estenssoro (formerly President of Bolivia then exiled in Lima, Peru) as well as other high officials— Bolivian and American—including the top general sent by the United States to help Bolivians catch and kill Ché Guevara.

10. Smith, Jane. "Fraser: Shah's Not in Hitler's Class." *Minneapolis Star*. Dec. 5, 1979. Section A. Part II. p. 17.

11. *Time*. "Nightmare in Jonestown." Dec. 4, 1978. pp. 16–27.

12. McCarthy, Colman. *Saint Paul Pioneer Press & Dispatch*. June 23, 1979.

12a. In commendable literature we can cite the actions of "good" people (Per Hansa, for example) who are not above "removing survey stakes" for their own benefit. Rölvaag O.E. *Giants of the Earth*. Harper & Row. New York 1955. pp. 117–121; See also *King's Row* by Henry Bellamann, where we see the "Main Street" people performing incest and needless cruelties to advance their own pleasures and ambitions. Simon & Shuster. New York. 1942.

13. See above p. 5–6.

14. Freud, Sigmond. *Moses and Monotheism*. Vintage Books. 1955. p. 68.

15. Feuerback, Ludvig Andreas. *Lecture on Essence of Religion*. (Frans Ralph Manheim) Harper & Row. New York. 1967. p. 50.

16. Feuerback. *Lecture*. p. 17.
17. See above, p. 28.

Chapter V

1. Dussel. *Theology of Liberation*. pp. 4–6.
2. Exodus 10:2, also 1–12.
3. Bonino, José Miguez. *Doing Theology in a Revolutionary Situation*. (Confrontation Books) Fortress Press. Philadelphia: Pa. 1975. p. 43ff.
4. *Ibid*., Foreword p. xivff; Dussel. *Theology of Liberation* pp. 32–33.
5. Küng, Hans. *On Being A Christian*. Doubleday & Co., Inc. Garden City, New York. (Trans. by Edward Quinn) 1968. pp. 29ff.
6. Dussel. *Theology of Liberation*. p. 8.
7. Perkins, Dexter. *Hands Off: A History of the Monroe Doctrine*. Little Brown & Co. Boston. 1952. Preface; Morison and Commager. *Growth of American People*. Vol I. p. 422.
8. Quoted in Dozer, Donald. *The Monroe Doctrine*. Knopf. Borzoi Books on Latin America. Preface.
9. Morison & Commager. *Growth of American People* Vol. I. p. 422.
10. See above, p. 40–41
11. Revolution usually signifies a basic change in society. Johnson, Chalmers. *Revolution and the Social System*. Stanford Univ. 1964. p. 2.
12. Parkes, Henry B. *A History of Mexico*. Houghton Mifffin & Co. Boston. 1950. p. 250.
13. *Ibid*., p. 273ff.
14. Hauberg, C.A. *Latin American Revolutions*. T.S. Denison. Minneapolis, Minn. 1968. p. 15; Crow, John C. *Mexico Today*. Harper. 1957. p. 135ff.
15. Parkes. *History of Mexico*. p. 332ff.
16. Hauberg. *Revolutions*. p. 25.
17. *Ibid*. Quoted on p. 29.
18. D'Antonio, William and Pike, Frederich B. (Eds.) *Religion, Revolution and Reform (New Forces for Change in Latin America)*. New York. Praeger. 1964.
19. Quoted in Hauberg, C. A. *Latin American Revolution*. T.S. Denison & Co. p. 40. 1968.
20. Hauberg. *Revolutions*. p. 41ff.
21. Alegría, Ciro, Farrar & Rinehart, Inc. New York & Toronto. 1941. pp. 20, 53, 163, 183, 433 and Chapter 7 and the last chapter, entitled "Whither? Whither?"
22. Figures quoted in Hauberg. *Revolutions*. p. 12.
23. D'Antonia & Pike. *Religion, Reform*. pp. 28–30.
24. Dussel. *Theology of Liberation*. pp. 18, 150–151, 265.
25. Bonino. *Doing Theology*, p. 2 or Chapter I, "Beyond Colonial & Neocolonial Christianity."
26. See above, p. 48 and Chapter IV, Notes 8a, 9.
27. Küng, *On Being a Christian*. p. 186.
28. *Ibid*., p. 83.

29. Riviere, William. *A Pastor Looks at Kierkegaard*. Zandervan Publishing House. Grand Rapids, Mich. p. 15.

30. Feuerback, *Essence of Religion*. p. 60.

31. Bonino. *Doing Theology*. p. 28.

32. Dussel. *Theology of Liberation*. pp. 117–118.

33. Hauberg. "Secondary Education Today," *Current History*. July, 1961. pp. 41–48.

34. This beginning is probably the real source of "*Cuba sí Yankee no!*"

35. Hauberg. *Revolutions*. The above specific accounts are found on pp. 196–98, but the whole story of Cuba as told here is covered between pp. 181–252.

36. Hauberg. *Revolutions*. p. 213, 232.

37. *Ibid.*, p. 244.

38. MacKay, John H. "Cuba Revisited." *Christian Century*. Feb. 12, 1964; Hauberg. *Revolutions*. pp. 181–252.

39. Freud, Sigmund, *Civilization, War and Death*. Hogarth Press, Ltd. London, 1953. pp. 80–81.

4. Ibid.

41. Edwards, *Debate*. p. 273.

42. Küng, *On Being a Christian*. p. 43–46.

43. See above p. 4.

44. Leonhard, Wolfgang. *Three Faces of Marxism*. Holt, Rinehart and Winston. New York, 1974, pp. 3, 18, 43–44.

45. Bonino, *Doing Theology*. Chapter I; Dussel, *Theology of Liberation*. Chapter IV.

46. *Lutheran Standard*. "The Front Page" March 4, 1980. June 15, 1980.

47. *Washington Spectator*. June 15, 1978. pp. 1–3.

48. *Ibid.*

49. Cronon, David. *Josephus Daniels in Mexico*. University of Wisconsin Press. Madison. 1960. pp. 13, 111, 203, 217.

50. Fuentes, Carlos. *El Augumento de Latino America (Palabras a Los Norte Americanos)*. April 13, 1962. pp. 21–23.

51. Eder, Richard. "Iran Today Seems Like Mexico in 1915." *Minneapolis Tribune*. Monday, January 14, 1980. p. 6A.

52. Paz, Octavio. *Labyrinth of Solitude*. (Translated by Lysander Kemp.) Evergreen Books Ltd. New York. 1961. p. 194.

AUTHOR'S NOTE: See also *The Sword and the Cross*, by Alan Riding, pp. 3–8.

Addendum

1. *Washington Spectator*, August 15, 1979. p.1–2; August 1, 1980, p. 4.

Bibliography

Books

Algeria, Ciro. *Broad and Alien Is the World*. New York: Farrar & Rinehart Inc., 1941.

Ault, Warren O. *Europe in the Middle Ages*. New York: D.C. Heath & Co., 1932.

Barth, Karl. *Christmas*. Edenburgh, London: Oliver & Boyd, 1959.

Bellamann, Henry. *King's Row*. New York: Simon & Schuster, 1942.

Bonhoeffer, Dietrich. *Act of Being*. New York: Harpter & Brothers Publishers, 1961.

Bonino, José Miguez. *Doing Theology in a Revolutionary Situation*. Philadelphia: Fortress Press, 1975.

Breasted, James H. *The Dawn of Conscience*. New York: Charles Scribner's Sons, 1933.

Bronowski, Jacob. *The Ascent of Man*. Boston: Little Brown & Co., 1974.

Cairns, David. *A Gospel Without Myth*. (Buttman's Challenge to the Preacher). London: S.C.M. Press Ltd., 1960.

Carroll, Lewis. *The Annotated Alice: Alice's Adventures in Wonderland and Through the Looking Glass*. Edited by Martin Gardner. Bramhall House.

CBS News. *Almanac 1978*. rev. ed. Edited by Martin A. Bachellor et al. Maplewood, New Jersey: Hammond Inc. & CBS News, 1978.

Dante, Aleghieri. *The Divine Comedy*. The Harvard Classics.

D'Antonio, William V., and Pike, Fredrick B. eds. *Religion, Revolution, and Reform: New Forces for Change in Latin America*. New York: Frederick A. Praeger, 1964.

Diffie, Bailly W. *Latin American Civilization*. Harrisburg, Pennsylvania: Stackpole Sons, 1945.

Dussel, Enrique. *History and the Theology of Liberation*. Maryknoll, New York: Orbis Books, 1976.

Edwards, David L., ed. *The Honest to God Debate: Some Reactions to the Book "Honest to God."* Philadelphia: The Westminister Press, 1963.

Feuerback, Ludwig Andreas. *Lecture on the Essence of Religion*. Translated by Ralph Manheim. New York: Harper & Row Publishers, 1967.

Feuerback, Ludwig Andreas. *The Essence of Faith According to Luther*. Translated by Melvin Cherno. New York: Harper & Row Publishers, 1967.

Fielding, Henry. *The History of Tom Jones*. (A Millar, London-4th printing 1750). Edited by Sheridan Baker. New York: W. W. Norton & Co., Inc., 1973.

Freud, Sigmund. *The Basic Writings of Sigmund Freud*. Edited by A. A. Brill.

New York: The Modern Library, 1938.
Freud, Sigmund. *Civilization, War and Death*. London: Hogarth Press, Ltd., 1953.
Freud, Sigmund. *Moses and Monotheism*. New York: Vintage Books, 1955.
Galbraith, John K. *The Affluent Society*. Boston: Houghton Mifflin Co., 1958.
George, Alexander L. and George, Juliette L. *Woodrow Wilson and Colonel House: A Personality Study*. New York: Dover Publications, Inc., 1964.
Gilkes, Patrick. *The Dying Lion*. London: T. Julian Friedman Publishers Ltd., 1975.
Greene, Felix. *A Curtain of Ignorance: How the American Public Has Been Misinformed about China*. Garden City, New York: Doubleday & Co., Inc., 1964.
Harrison, Bernard. *Henry Fielding's Tom Jones*. Sussex University Press, 1975.
Hart, Bernard. *The Psychology of Insanity*. New York: The MacMillan Co., 1937.
Hauberg, Clifford H. *Latin American Revolutions*. Minneapolis, Minnesota: T. S. Denison & Co., Inc., 1968.
Hayes, Carlton J. H. *A Political and Cultural History of Modern Europe*. [Vol. I, 1500–1830; Vol. II, since 1830.] New York: MacMillan & Co.
Hanke, Lewis. *Aristotle and The American Indians*: A Study in Race Prejudice in the Modern World. Bloomington, Indiana: Indiana University Press, 1959.
Heaton, Herbert. *Economic History of Europe*. New York: Harper & Brothers, 1936.
Herring, Hubert. *A History of Latin America*. 3rd ed. New York: Alfred A. Knopf, 1961.
Hoffer, Eric. *The True Believer: Thoughts on the Nature of Mass Movements*. New York: Harper & Brothers, 1951.
Holy Bible (Old and New Testament) Edited by American Revision Committee. standard revised edition. New York: Thomas Nelson and Sons, 1946.
Kung, Hans. *On Being A Christian*. Translated by Edward Irwin. Garden City, New York: Doubleday & Co., Inc., 1976.
Leonard, Wolfgang. *Three Faces of Marxism*. New York & Chicago: Holt, Rinehard & Winston, 1974.
The Living Bible, Carmel, New York: Gundeposts Associates, Inc., 1971.
Lunt, W. E. *History of England*. New York: Harper & Brothers, 1938.
Lucas, Henry S. *The Rennaisance and the Reformation*. New York: Harpers & Brothers, 1934.
Luscombe, D. E. *Peter Abelard's Ethics*. Oxford: Claredon Press, 1971.
Marcuse, Herbert. *One Dimensional Man: Studies in the Ideology of Advanced Industrial Society*. Boston: Beacon Press, 1964.
The New English Bible. (With the Apocrypha). Oxford Study edition. Oxford University Press, 1976.
Niebuhr, Reinhold. *Justice and Mercy*. Edited by Ursula Niebuhr. New York: Harper & Row Publishers, 1974.
Northrop F. S. C. *The Meeting of East and West*. New York: The MacMillan Co., 1947.
Niebuhr, Richard H. *The Responsible Self: An Essay in Christian Moral Philosophy*. New York: Harper & Row, 1963.
MacKinney, Loren Carey. *The Medieval World*. New York: Rinehart & Co., Inc., 1947.

Morrison, S. E. and Commager, H. S. *The Growth of the American Republic.* New York: Oxford University Press, vol. 1 & 2., 1942.
Omar Khayyam. *The Rubaiyat.* London: Dodge Publishing Company (Fitzgerald Edition), 1914.
The Oxford Annoted Bible (with Apocrypha II). Edited by Herbert G. Mag and Bruce M. Melzger. Oxford: Oxford University Press, 1965.
Parkes, Henry Bamford. *A History of Mexico.* Boston: Houghton Mifflin Co., 1950.
Paz, Octavio. *Labyrith of Solitude: Life and Thought in Mexico.* New York: Grove Press, Inc., 1921.
Phillips, J. B. *Appointment with God.* New York: The MacMillan Co., 1954.
Phillips, J. B. *Your God is Too Small.* New York: The MacMillan Co., 1953.
Pike, James A. *A Time for Christian Candor.* New York: Harper & Row, 1964.
Redmond, Howard A. *The Omnipotence of God.* Philadelphia: The Westminister Press, 1946.
Reviere, William T. *A Pastor Looks at Kierkegaard.* Grand Rapids, Michigan: Zonerman Publishing House.
Robinson, John A. *Honest to God.* Philadelphia: The Westminister Press, 1963.
Rolvag, O. E. *Giants in the Earth.* New York: Harper & Row Publishers, 1927.
Scheper-Hughes, Nancy. *Saints, Scholars & Schizophrenics: Mental Illness in Rural Ireland.* Berkeley, California: University of California Press, 1979.
Sikes, J. G. *Peter Abailard.* New York: Russell & Russell, Inc., 1964.
Stearns, Raymond Phineas. *Pageant of Europe.* New York: Harcourt & Brace & Co., 1947.
Taylor, H. O. *Thought and Expression of the 17th Century.* New York: MacMillan and Co., 1920.
Trevelzan, George H. *Lord Gray and the Reform of Bill.* London, 1920.
Tuckman, Barbara W. *A Distant Mirror: The Calmitous 14th Century.* New York: Alfred Knopf, 1978.
Viscott, David S., M.D. *The Making of a Psychiatrist.* New York: Arbor House, 1972.

Encyclopedias

Edwards, Paul ed. *The Encyclopedia of Philosophy.* New York: MacMillan and the Free Press, 1961.
Dictionary of National Biography. Vol. XIII. Edited by Sir Leslie Stephen and Sir Sidney Lee. Oxford: Oxford University Press,
Dictionary of American Biography, VI., Edited by Allen Johnson and Dumas Malone. New York: Charles Scribner & Sons, 1931.
World Book Encyclopedia. Field Enterprises Inc., 18 Vols. Chicago, Ill.

Newspapers and Periodicals

St. Paul Pioneer Press & Dispatch, St. Paul, Minnesota.
Minneapolis Tribune, 425 Portland Avenue, Minneapolis, Minnesota.

Minneapolis Star, 425 Portland Avenue, Minneapolis, Minnesota.
New Republic, Editor in Chief, Marlin Peretz, Farmington, NY 11737.
Time, James R. Shepley, President, 541 N. Fairbank Street, Chicago, Illinois
Washington Spectator (and *Between the Lines*), Editor Tristram Coffin, PO Box 32280, Washington, D.C.

Index

Abelard, Peter, 4, 19, 26
Abraham, 17
Alice, 5
Allende, Salvador, 48, 49
American Observer, 2
Amin, Idi, of Uganda, 50
Andrew, Apostle, 16
Anselm, 26
Arians, 22
Azuelo, Mariano, 63

Babel, story of, 20
Bacon, Roger, 26
Barrabas, 17
Barth, Karl, 12
Batista y Zaldivar, Fulgencio, 69–70
Benedictines, 24
Boers, 42
Bonhoeffer, Dietrich, 12
Bonino, Jose Miguez, 68
Bonsal, Philip, 71
Borlaug, Norman E., 7
Brahe, Tycho, 20
Brazil, 68
Breasted, James H., 72
Broad and Alien Is the World, 65
Brown, Robert, and followers, 31 ff.

Cairns, David, 19
Calderon, Battle of, 59
Calles, Plutarco Elias, 14, 64, 74
Calvin, John, 20, 29
Camara, Dom Helder, 68
Carrangza, Venustiano, 63, 64
Cardenas, Lazaro, 65, 70, 74, 75, 76
Carroll, Lewis, 2, 5
Castro, Fidel, 70, 71, 74
Catholicism, 21 ff.
Caudillo, 60, 61
Central Intelligence Agency (C.I.A.), 48, 49
Charles IV of Spain, 59
Chaucer, Geoffrey. See Note 86
Chavez, Cesar, 66
Chilean story, 48–49
Christendom, 4, 34 ff., 42, 48 ff., 50, 56, 64, 75
Christology, 15 (*see* Note 11), 34 ff., 84, 50, 53, 56
Christianity, 4, 8, 13, 18, 21 ff., 34, 36, 39, 41, 52, 67
Ciardi, John, 4
Clark, Ramsey, 50
Clausewitz, Karl Von, 3
Clawson, Lilac, 74
Colonialism
  Old, and Christendom, 57 ff.
  Neo-, and Christendom, 57 ff., 68
Commager, Henry S., 5
Copernicus, 20, 4
Confucius, 18
Cortés, Hernán and the Conquistadores, 40 ff.
Council of Nicaea, 22
Crime of Anagni, 24 ff., 31
Cromwell, Oliver, 32
Cronon, David, 75
Cuba, 9, 69–71

Cuban Constitution of 1940, 70
Cultural lag, 1

Daniels, Josephus, 71, 75, 76
Descartes, Rene, 17
Diaz, Porfirio, 60–62
Diffie, Bailey W., 41
Dante, Alighieri, 27, 51
Dewey, Admiral, 76
Divine Right of Kings, 29 ff., 30, 32, 86, Note 41
Dostoyevsky, Feodor Mikhailovich, 5
Dr. Jekyll–Mr. Hyde Personality, 46
Dulles, John Foster, 9
Dussel, Enrique, 41, 55, 67

Eddy, Margaret Baker
and the Monroe Doctrine, 57–58
Edwards, David L., 12
Edwards, Jonathan, 12 ff.
Einstein, Albert, 3
Elizabeth I, 31
Engler, Robert, 8
Enlightenment, 2, 11, 57, 58, 64, 65, 72, 81
Erasmus, Disederius, 27 ff.
Ego, Marie, 74
Exodus, 20, 55

Ferdinand of Aragon, 39
Fraser, Donald, 49 ff.
Fuentes, Carlos, story of, 76–77
Freud, Sigmund, 12
Feuerback, Ludwig, A., 12, 53, 67

Gabriel, 15
Galileo, 4, 20
Gandhi Mahatama, 57
George III, King, 44
Geyer, Georgie Anne, 46
God, 28, 50, 53, 54, 55, 56 ff., 68, 73
Gospels, 15
Graham, Billy, 51 ff.
Greene, Felix, 4, 73
Grito de Dolorés, 59
Guevara, Ernesto (Ché), 67

Hart, Bernard, 44–46, Note 5 (ch. 4)
Hayes, Carlton J., 2
Heaton, Herbert, 24
Helsinki and Salt Agreements, 79
Henry VIII, 31
Herod, 15
Herring, Hubert, 40, Note 9 (p. 86)
Hidalgo y Costilla, Father Miguel, 59
Hilter, Adolf, 31
Hoffer, Eric, 18, Note 16 (p. 85)
Holmes, Oliver H., 5
Holy Roman Empire, 27
Huerta, Victorio, 62
Humpty-Dumpty, 5
Hugo, Victor, 61
Humanism, 28, 68

Imperialism, 35, 64, 65–66, 72
Insanity, 44 ff.
Isabella of Castile, 39
Islam, 36
Iturbide, Augustin de, 59

Joseph of Nazareth, 15
Jalisco, Archbishop of, 14, 64
Jehovah, 19, 55
Jesuits, 42
Jesus Christ, 6, 15 ff., 16, 17, 20 ff., 34, 50, 51, 56, 65, 67, 68
Jones, Jim, 50
Jones, Tom, 20
John the Baptist, 16
John, King, 24
Johnson, Lyndon, 51
Juarez, Benito
and La Reforma, 60 ff.
Judas Iscariot, 16
Julius Caesar, 44

Kepler, Johann, 20
Khomeini, Ayotollah, of Iran, 46 ff.
Kierkegaard, Sören, 12, 67
King, Martin Luther, Jr., 57
Krey, August C., 24
Küng, Hans, 67, 62

Las Casas, Bartoleme de, 40, 58

Lazarus, 13
Lewin Nikalai, 72, 73
Lewis, Oscar, 63
Liberation Theology, 18, 43, 55 ff.
Lincoln, Abraham, 61
Lippman, Walter, 68
Locke, John, 32
Los reyes Catolicos, 39
Lot, 19
Luther, Martin, 20, 27 ff., 29, 30 ff., 57, 67, 68

Marx, Karl
and Marxism, 50, 72, 73
Machado, Gerardo, 69
Madero, Francisco I, 62
Mahan, Alfred Thayer, 3
Mann, Ambassador, 76
Marina, Doña, 40
Matthew, 18
McCarthy, Joseph
and McCarthyism, 9, 10, 72
McIntyre, Senator Thomas, 9
McKinley, William, 43
Medici, Lorenzo de, 26
Methodist, 5
Mexican Constitution of 1917, 63, 64
Mexican War, 60
oil problem, 75
Mill, John Stuart, 81
Missile Crisis, 71
Mohammedanism, 36 ff.
Monroe Doctrine, 57 ff.
Montalva, Edwardo Frei, 66
Montesinos, Antonio de and the Clergy, 40, 58
Moors, 36 ff., Note 3 (p. 86)
Morelos, José Maria, 59
Morgenthau, Hans J., 3
Moses, 55
Moslems, 47 ff.

National Revolutionary Party, 65, 74
Nationalism, 24, 27, 29, 30, 31, 39
Narváez, Panfilo de, 40
Niebuhr, Reinhold, 12
Nelson, Donald M., 1
Nixon, Richard, 51
Northrup, F.S.C., 25
Nuclear Items, 3, 74

"Oak Ridge" for Peace, 78
Obregón, Alvaro, 64
Odoacer, 23
Omar, Khayyam, 14, 64
Organization of American States (O.A.S.), 49, 71

Pandora's Box, 33
Paul, Apostle of the Gentiles, 21 ff.
Paz, Octavio, 58, 77
Pazzi, Plot, 26
Peasant's Revolt of 1524, 29, 35
Pelagian, 25
Pelayo and the Reconquista, 38
Peter, Apostle, 16, 21 ff.
Petrarch, Fransisco, 27, 28, 57
Petrine Doctrine, 22, 23, 34
Philip IV of France, 24
Phillips, J. B., 4, 12
Pharisees, 16
Pico della Mirandola, 28, 53
Pike, James, 12, 19, 20, 43
Pinochet, (General) Augusto, 48
Platt Amendment, 69, 76
Plato, 13, 36
Pollard, A. F., 4
Pontius Pilate, 16
Popes
Boniface VIII 1294–1303, 25, 51
Celestine V 1294, 51
Gregory the Great 540–704, Note 32 (p. 85)
Gregory VII 1073–1086, 35
Innocent III 1198–1216, 24 ff., 35
John XXII 1316–1334, 53, Note 33
John XXIII 1958–1963, 57
John Paul II 1978, 35
Leo X 1513–1522, 25, 30, 35
Sixtus IV 1471–1484, 26 ff., 35
Urban II, 37
Portillo, Lopéz, 77
Pringler, Henry F., 6
Puritans, 31

Rather, Dan, 79
Reconquista, 36, 38 ff.
Redmond, Howard A., 13 ff.
Protestant Reformation, 27–33
Reform Bill of 1832 (Great Britain), 42
Renaissance, 27 ff.
Richard, King, Coeur de Lion, 37 ff.
Robinson, John, A.T., 11 ff., 19, 20
Romans, 36
Roosevelt, F. D., 75
Rubaiyat, 14, 64
Ryan, Leo, 50

Sadat, Anwar, 47
St. Anselm, 26
St. Bernard, 28, 411 ff.
Saladin and Third Crusade, 37
Sanity, 44 ff.
Santa Anna Antono López de, 59 ff.
Santiago y a ellos, 38, 40
Sarai and Abran, 19
Sarajno Incident, 79
Saudi Arabia, 48
Savak, 49
Scholastics, 13, 14, 26, 27, 28, 64
Scientology, 50 ff., 52
Second Vatican Council, 7
Sermon on the Mount, 16, 20
Shah of Iran, Mohammed Reza Pahlavi, 9 ff., 49
Sixty Minutes, 49–50, 79
Socrates, 4
Stalin, Joseph V., 72, 73
Stuarts and the Fall of the Divine Right of Kings Idea in England, 32 ff.

Tours, Battle of, 36
Tarik, 36 see FN #4, 86, 47
Tennyson, Alfred, 28, 82
Tenochtitlán, 40
Tetzel, John, 25
Texas, 60
Tillich, Paul, 12
Tito, Josip Broz, 73
Toleration Act of 1689, 32
Torres, Camilo, 56, 67
Trevelyan, G. M., 42
Tsongas, Paul E., 10

Unam Sanctum, 25
United Nations, 1, 71

Villa, Pancho, 63
Virgin Mary, 15
Viscott, David, 45
Vonnegut, Kurt, 82

Wallace, Mike, 79
Walpole, Robert, 32
Weizsächer, Carl Frederick von, 67
Whitehead, Alfred North, 68
Wilson, Henry Lane, 62, 63
Wycliffe, John, 27

Yemen, 48

Zapata, Emiliano, 63
Zumárraga, Juan de, 41, 58